REFLECTIONS

OF A JACOBITE

BY

LOUIS AUCHINCLOSS

The Indifferent Children

The Injustice Collectors

Sybil

A Law for the Lion

The Romantic Egoists

The Great World and Timothy Colt

Venus in Sparta

Pursuit of the Prodigal

The House of Five Talents

Reflections of a Jacobite

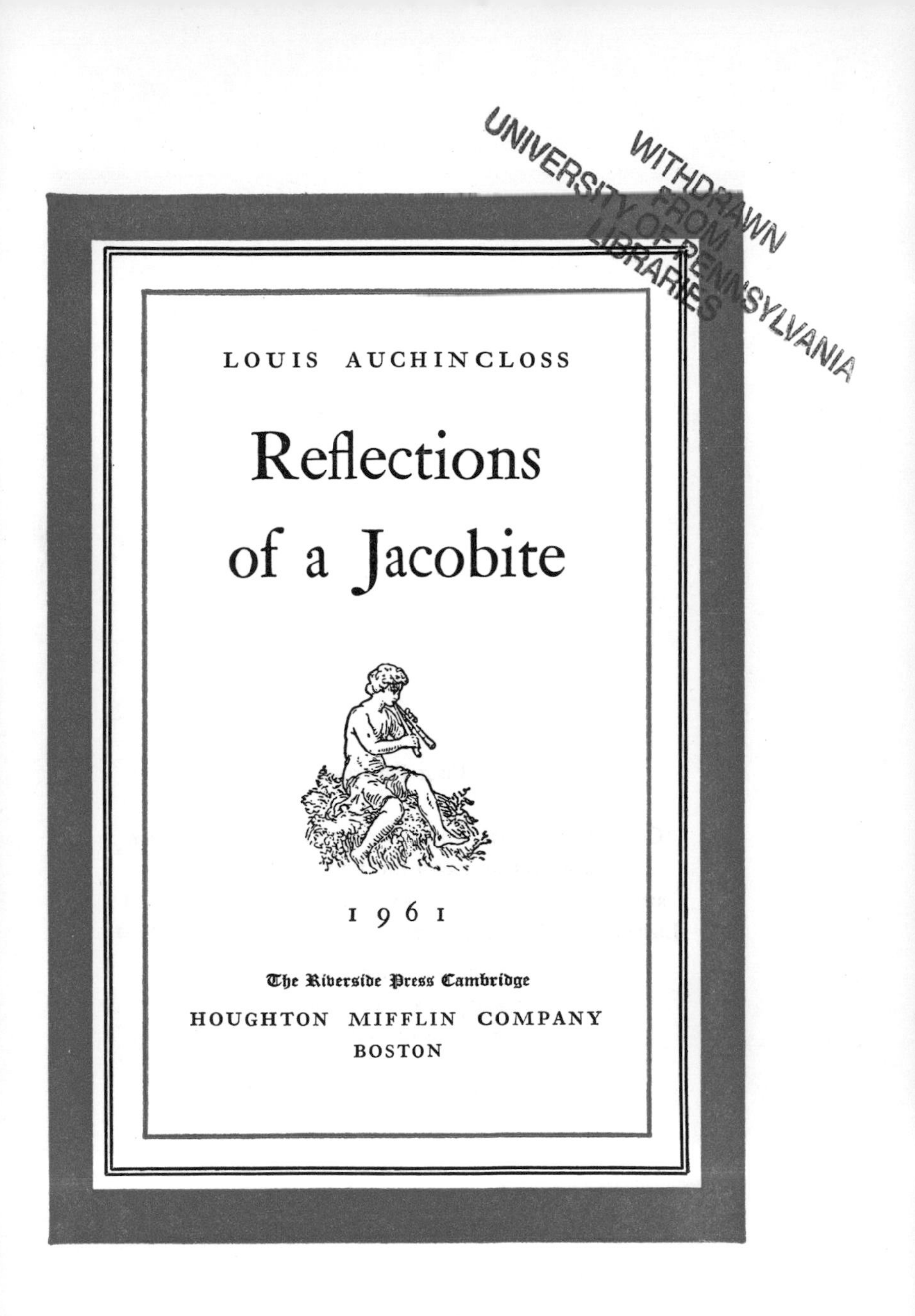

LOUIS AUCHINCLOSS

Reflections of a Jacobite

1961

The Riverside Press Cambridge
HOUGHTON MIFFLIN COMPANY
BOSTON

First Printing

Library of Congress Catalog Card Number: 61-8700

The Riverside Press
CAMBRIDGE • MASSACHUSETTS
PRINTED IN THE U.S.A.

For Father and Mother

on their golden wedding anniversary

April 19, 1961

with all my love and gratitude and admiration

*

Acknowledgments

"Edith Wharton and Her New Yorks" and "Proust's Picture of Society" have previously appeared in *Partisan Review.*

"The Novel of Manners Today: Marquand and O'Hara" and "A Reader's Guide to the Fiction of Henry James" first appeared in *The Nation.*

Foreword

I HAVE CALLED myself a Jacobite because so much of my lifetime's reading has been over the shoulder of Henry James. To follow the opinions scattered through his criticism, his letters, his memoirs, even his travel pieces, is to be conducted through the literature of his time, English, American, French and Russian, by a kindly guide of infinitely good manners, who is also infinitely discerning, tasteful and conscientious. It does not really matter whether one always agrees with him, whether, for example, one finds the Russian novels "fluid pudding" or Robert Louis Stevenson the first English writer of the nineties. All that matters is the prolonged opportunity to consider the fiction of his contemporaries through the clear eyes of a master novelist to whom the art of constructing stories was always a desperately serious one. James's long life, to a degree rare even among creative writers, was dedicated to and saturated in literature, from that early day in Washington Square, when a huge, benevolent Thackeray, calling on his father, had boomed down: "Come here, little boy, and show me your extraordinary jacket!" to the time, almost seventy years later, when Edith Wharton sent him *Swann's Way*, and he knew at once that they had turned a page in the history of the novel.

I do not profess in this little book to study James as a critic, or even, except briefly, as a novelist. It is rather that he provides me with my starting point and my common denominator. If it were not presumptuous, I would call him my master of ceremonies. Of the authors whom I discuss, he was a close friend of Edith Wharton and Paul Bourget, a good friend of Daudet and Meredith, a familiar acquaintance of Trollope and George Eliot, and, as a child, had been called "Buttons" by Thackeray himself. It is not clear that he ever knew Proust, though Lucien Daudet remembered a lunch in Paris where both were present. I have added a few authors unknown to James, but wherever possible, I have left it to the master to make my introductions.

I want to offer my thanks to Leon Edel, the unquestioned authority on James's life and letters, and indeed on all of the master's work, for his kind help in supplying me with information and suggestions. I am but an acolyte at the altar where he is high priest.

Louis Auchincloss

Contents

REFLECTIONS OF A JACOBITE

Early Reading and Alphonse Daudet

FOR A PERSON who has derived so much of his pleasure in life reading novels, I came to it surprisingly late. It was not until my war service in the Navy that I began to read fiction in any quantity with no aim but that of enjoying it. It was escapism, of course, the sheerest escapism, but who but a Churchill would not be an escapist in wartime? As I look back on those long years in the Atlantic and Pacific, the oceans seem linked in my mind by the isthmus of the Victorian novel. I associate the atolls of Ulithi and Eniwetok with Barsetshire and Mrs. Proudie and the amphibious-training base at Camp Bradford, Virginia, with *The Spoils of Poynton.* Nothing else stood by me so well in that time of spasmodic anxiety and prolonged boredom.

It was not, of course, that I began to read in the war, but that I began to enjoy reading. At boarding school I considered myself very literary indeed, but I cannot recall much actual pleasure from books. I read for marks. So serious a business was not to be confused with anything as trivial as pleasure. I burned to make up in academic pre-eminence what I lacked in athletic prowess and popularity, and I looked on books as mere rungs in the ladder of fame, much as a man in the Middle Ages, discouraged with his prospects on the battlefield, might look to a church career for political advancement. The pages of Dickens and Thackeray existed only to be squeezed through the mental grinder that would turn them into grades. My teachers made efforts to improve my standard of values, but what can adults accomplish against the obsessions of a boy? It took a world conflagration to teach me what books were for.

My first glimmering, however, that the reading of fiction might play a nonutilitarian role came before the war, at Yale, in a French course. I do not mean to disparage my English professors, who were all gifted men, but the identification between Shakespeare and the Phi Beta Kappa key was too close to my heart for them to unravel. The French novel, on the other hand, except for *Colomba* and *Le Crime de Sylvestre Bonnard*, was unknown to me until Joseph Seronde's lectures in nineteenth century French literature. Balzac and Stendhal had not been confused with my personal ambition, and I was fascinated to learn how passionately the French public had sided for or against the new trends of the century: romanticism, naturalism, realism. It was my first glimpse of a society where literature was the concern of someone besides teachers and students. I had been brought up to view the world as a more serious affair. I could not imagine my own father or the fathers of any of my friends donning red vests at the opening of *Hernani.* My mother used even to ridicule a college education that consisted so largely of reading novels. It was not that she disapproved of novels — she was and is a voracious reader of them — but she believed that they were intended to provide diversion rather than education. She thought that courses for young men who would have to live in a troubled world should be in science or philosophy or economics. I could and still can understand her point of view. It does seem a bit curious to have to "study" such thrillers as *Jane Eyre* or *Tess of the d'Urbervilles.* But the fact remains that the reading taste established by Joseph Seronde was the most concrete thing that I bore away from Yale and that it has given me more lasting pleasure than I can possibly imagine that I would have received from any course in economics. Yale and French nineteenth century literature will always be bracketed in my mind.

The novel, despite its author's declining reputation, that made the deepest impression on me in sophomore year was *Fromont Jeune et Risler Aîné.* I suppose that no one would rank Daudet today with Flaubert or the Goncourts or Zola, who were in life his friends and admirers. He is among the great casualties of our era, like George Eliot and Howells. But some casualties are caused simply by the growing bulk of our literature. It is impossible to admire every novelist who is admirable. If a writer survives, we keep all of him; we save *The Sacred Fount* with James and *Titus Andronicus* with Shakespeare. We write learned theses in defense of minor works and reprint them with enticing paper covers. But when a writer falls from grace, we tend to pitch all his books after him, except in rare cases like *Cranford* or *Lorna Doone.* It seems a pity that the best of Daudet should be less read than the least of Stendhal.

Fromont came to me at a good time, for I was reacting against an overdose of Dickens. Daudet is a softer, mellower Dickens; there is less smell of grease paint, less glare of footlights. His characters are never so exaggerated, for they are not creatures of fantasy but faithful reproductions of persons whom Daudet saw or knew. I imagine that every eccentric whom Dickens observed suggested an even greater eccentric to his imagination, while Daudet was content with the limitations of his model. Sometimes too content. He and his literary group made a fetish of accuracy in observed details. In his memoirs he relates that while writing *Fromont* he was warned that Dickens had already "done" a crippled doll dresser in *Our Mutual Friend.* For days he roamed the Marais, climbing stairways to look at signs, until he came upon the notice OISEAUX ET MOUCHES POUR MODES, and knew at once Désirée Delobelle's new trade. Daudet made less effort to conceal his sources of inspiration than any novelist before Thomas Wolfe. "It is sometimes a weakness of mine," he wrote, "to leave to my models their real names, and to persuade myself that were the name transformed, it would take away something from the integrity of the creation." One understands why he had so much trouble with his friends.

Fromont is full of the working life of the faubourgs, the straight smoke of the factories, the call bells, the rumble of vans and the rattle of handcarts, the noise of workmen entering and leaving the mills. Daudet, for all the meticulousness of his research, paints his final picture with the brush of a contemporary impressionist. Yet behind the dust and roar of a mercantile Paris one has a sense of beauty and romance ready to burst out, like tough weeds between the cobblestones. Désirée may never leave her attic room where she models birds and flies for fashionable bonnets, but she has the image of Franz Risler to which she can escape, as the tradesmen escape on Sunday to a countryside of grass and flowers. The novel is richly, unabashedly sentimental, but it was a sentimentality that hit me just right in sophomore year. Perhaps I associated the Marais with the somber ugliness of an industrial New Haven and the bleakness of warehouses and machinery sheds by a grey, wintry Long Island Sound. And perhaps I found Daudet's alleviating sense of romance in the melancholy moodiness of nineteen.

I will admit that I have not found quite the same satisfaction in the other volumes of the *Moeurs Parisiennes*, read in later years. It seems to me that their plots are too rambling, their heroes too crushed by circumstance. And when I last turned back to *Fromont*, I wondered if I would find it like the others, beautiful but damp. I wondered how much of my early enthusiasm had been due to youth, and I remembered Proust's warning never to reread one's old favorites, but simply to finger the old editions and evoke the memories with which they are associated. I decided, however, to take the risk, and I was rewarded. After twenty years I found the old charm still there, and the struggle between the good and wicked forces over the paper factory as entrancing as ever.

The factory, around which the plot revolves, is in the Marais, closely hemmed in by shops and tenements. Near it is the elegant residence and garden of the proprietor. The different social strata of the industry are thus brought into the closest juxtaposition: the factory and house, symbols, respectively, of the production of money and its expenditure, become the center of a staring, envious world that has too much to do with the first and too little with the second. Risler, a good man, has eyes only for the factory where he hopes to obtain a modest success by hard toil, but Sidonie Chèbe sighs yearningly over the house and garden which she plans, at any cost, to make her own. Thus the basic conflict is announced, between those who recognize the true function of industry and those who hanker only for its fruits, between the workers and the parasites. When Risler and Sidonie marry, as they do in the very first chapter, there is a fusion of the two ambitions, the good and the bad.

The good will win out, but it will *just* win out. That is what happens in Daudet. The factory will manage to survive the ultimate exposure and humiliation of Sidonie, but Désirée and Risler will be suicides, and Claire Fromont will know her husband for the sorry creature that he is. The cancer is excised, and the victim will live, but the house of Fromont Jeune and Risler Ainé may expect some rocky months and years to come.

Of course it is a melodramatic tale. Of course it is sentimental. There are passages about Désirée as florid as anything Dickens wrote about Little Nell. But I still find it honest. Claire Fromont may be described as a real and Sidonie as a false pearl, but Claire is by no means the faultless heroine that she might have been, conceived across the Channel. Claire's obsessive concern with her little daughter is one of the reasons for her husband's derelictions, as Risler's obstinate immersion in his business is one for Sidonie's. The good people in Daudet are to blame for their willful blindness; they invite betrayal like those who leave open purses about. Risler, particularly, seems almost to deserve his wretched fate. He forfeits our sympathy by his gullibility until he rises to his magnificent revenge. When he looms up at Sidonie's party and thunders: "Madame Risler!", when he throws her and her jewels at Claire's feet and forces her to crave the pardon of her bitterest enemy, is it splendid drama? Or is it corn?

How can one always tell? When I read, as one so often does, of the "nature of evil" in modern fiction, I wonder if it is a complex or a very simple idea. Sometimes there is a good deal of obfuscating discussion of white whales or the ghosts of governesses and valets, but sometimes, also, the critic seems to find the evil just where one might expect to find it — in selfish, dissipated characters. Might I not then assert that Daudet is interested in the nature of evil? Might it not serve to revive his old popularity? But I doubt it. Daudet tried too hard to please. As James says:

> There is something very hard, very dry, in Flaubert, in Edmond de Goncourt, in the robust Zola; but there is something very soft in Alphonse Daudet. "Benevolent nature," says Zola, "has placed him at the exquisite point where poetry ends and reality begins." This is happily said; Daudet's great characteristic is this mixture of the sense of the real with the sense of the beautiful.

Daudet leads his reader through a wilderness which his prose turns into a garden. He tried to be as good a realist as his friends, the Goncourts, and indeed, much of his subject matter is as unlovely to the eye and nose. The hero of *Jack*, chronically drunk and coughing out his lungs in the boiler room of a ship, or the prostitute in *Sapho*, turning into an unkempt harridan, are as minutely observed as the alcoholic doctor of *Soeur Philomène* or the disintegrating chambermaid of *Germinie Lacerteux*. But Daudet is not so stern about his art; he is not so anxious to show off the accuracy of his note-taking. He did not believe that suffering exists only to be described by writers of the naturalist school. Daudet loved Paris, even the poorest sections of it. He did not have to escape, like the Goncourts, when not engaged in naturalist fiction, into boudoir history of the eighteenth century. He did not need the fantasy life of making inventories of the bric-à-brac of Madame de Pompadour or Madame du Barry. Even Flaubert went from Madame Bovary to the exotic scenes of ancient Carthage. When Daudet needed the picturesque, he brought his *Nabob* to the Paris of his own time. And when he took his readers on excursions to scenes of injustice and suffering, he brought a heart that, however sentimental, had still its core of true feeling. He believed that it was the function of a guide to entertain as well as instruct. But I wonder if modern readers are not more in the mood of the Goncourts. I doubt if they want their wildernesses tampered with. They pay, after all, for the "real thing."

Edith Wharton and Her New Yorks

THE CORRESPONDENCE, and, no doubt, the conversations between Henry James and Edith Wharton, were carried on in the happy tone of hyperbole. It was the pose of each to appear to grovel obsequiously before the other's superiority. She professed to regard him as the master of her art, the wise, benignant guide and mentor, while he likened her to a golden eagle with a beautiful genius for great globe adventures, at whose side he was nothing but "a poor old croaking barnyard fowl." "I have simply lain stretched," he wrote her, on hearing of a motor trip in Tunisia, "a faithful old veteran slave, upon the door-mat of your palace of adventure." Yet, as is often the case in such relationships, beneath the elaborate encomiums lay a vein of hidden mockery, almost, at times, of smugness. He really thought that she was dissipating her energy and talents, while she never doubted that he was hoarding his. And neither appreciated the other's best work.

She found his later novels "more and more lacking in atmosphere, more and more severed from that thick nourishing human air in which we all live and move." Everything in them had to be fitted into a predestined design, and design, to Edith Wharton, was "one of the least important things in fiction." James, on the other hand, found her at her best when most under his influence, and considered her finest work that mild little tale, *The Reef*, where a group of sensitive, cultivated expatriates in a French château are reduced to quiet desperation by the discovery that one of them has had an affair with the governess. There are passages that read like a parody of James himself:

> "I want to say — Owen, you've been admirable all through."
>
> He broke into a laugh in which the odd elder-brotherly note was once more perceptible.
>
> "Admirable," she emphasized. "And so has *she*."
>
> "Oh, and so have you to *her!*" His voice broke down to boyishness.

Yet the master found it all of a "psychological Racinian unity, intensity and gracility." The only thing that he questioned was why the characters, all American, should have elected to have their story carried out in France, and he warned her of the dangers of living abroad, with a wry little touch of humor at his own expense:

> Your only drawback is not having the homeliness and the inevitability and the happy limitation and the affluent poverty, of a Country of your Own (*comme moi, par exemple*)!

It was not the first time that he had sounded this warning. Ten years earlier, in 1902, he had written to her sister-in-law that she should be "tethered in native pastures, even if it reduces her to a backyard in New York." Viewed from the vantage point of today, with all of Mrs. Wharton's later novels before us that James never saw, the danger against which he warned her seems painfully obvious. It is difficult to read those slick satires about an America that she rarely bothered to visit without reflecting that she appeared, at the end, to have lost not only her country but her talent. What is curious, therefore, is that James should have foreseen this so clearly and yet should not have fully appreciated how much in 1902, and even as late as 1912, she still *had* a country, or at least a city, of her own. He may have been too out of touch with New York to appreciate how much she still belonged to it. Her ties, of course, were stronger than his. She had been brought up in the city and had married there. She had experienced its social life, in greater doses than she had wanted. She knew its men and women of property; she knew their history and their origins, their prejudices and ideals, the source of their money and how they spent their summers. This knowledge, of course, was eventually to fade with her continued residence abroad, but the ten years that preceded the first war were actually the years when her American impressions were at their most vivid and when she was doing her strongest work. It was the period of *The House of Mirth* and *The Custom of the Country*, the period when, true to her own vocation, she became the interpreter of certain aspects of New York life that she was uniquely qualified to describe.

The thing that was going on in Mrs. Wharton's New York of this period, and which she chose as the subject of her main study, was the assault upon an old and conservative group by the multitudes enriched, and fabulously enriched, by the business expansion of the preceding decades. The New York of the pre-assault era was the New York that she was later and nostalgically to describe in *The Age of Innocence*, the town of sober brownstone houses with high stoops, of an Academy of Music with shabby red and gold boxes, of long midday lunches with madeira, of husbands who never went "downtown," of a sense of precedence that was military in its strictness. As she tells us in her autobiography, when her grandmother's carriage appeared on Fifth Avenue those of her aunts maintained their proper distance in the rear. To this New York belong such of her characters as Mrs. Peniston, Lawrence Selden, the Peytons, the Dagonets, the Marvells, the van der Luydens. It was a city that was worldly beyond a doubt, but worldly with a sense of order and form, with plenty of leisure time in which art, music and literature could play a moderated role. The people from this world may lack strength of character, but their inertia is coupled with taste and observation, as seen in Lawrence Selden's parents:

> Neither one of the couple cared for money, but their disdain of it took the form of always spending a little more than was prudent. If their house was shabby, it was exquisitely kept; if there were good books on the shelves there were also good dishes on the table. Selden senior had an eye for a picture, his wife an understanding of old lace; and both were so conscious of restraint and discrimination in buying that they never quite knew how it was that the bills mounted up.

The young men practice law in a listless sort of way with much time for dining at clubs and trips to Europe. They have a settled sense of how their lives are to be led and no idea of impending change. The change, if change it really is, comes with the infiltration of the other protagonists of the drama, the Spraggs, the Wellington Brys, the Gormers, Sim Rosedale, the Van Osburghs, the Bryces, people who can spend a thousand dollars to Mrs. Peniston's one. Their assault on the brownstone citadel of old New York and its rapid capitulation provide a study of conflicting and ultimately reconciled types of snobbishness. The reconciliation is not altogether a surprise, for snobs *can* usually be reconciled. The old society may have had a brittle and varnished shell, but it covered a materialism as rampant as that of the richest parvenu. It could only be a matter of time before the new money was made to feel at home. Mrs. Wharton anticipated Proustian distinctions in her analysis of the different layers of the social hierarchy, but it is a dreary picture unrelieved by a Swann or a Charlus. From the top to the bottom of *The House of Mirth*, from Judy Trenor and "Bellomont," down through the pushing Brys and the false bohemianism of Mattie Gormer, to the "vast, gilded" hotel life of Norma Hatch, the entire fabric revolves around money.

Conflict is lost in fusion, which brings us to the deeper drama of *The House of Mirth*, the drama not of rival classes who drown their feud in noisy merger, but of their victims, those poor beings who are weak enough to care for the luxury, but too squeamish to play the game as roughly as it must be played. Lily Bart, of course, is the most famous of these. We see her first at the age of twenty-nine, beautiful, vivid but tired, regaining behind a veil that "purity of tint" that she is beginning to lose "after years of late hours and indefatigable dancing," waiting in Grand Central "in the act of transition between one and another of the country houses that disputed her presence at the close of the Newport season." But we are soon made aware of the sea of unpaid bills and small favors in which she precariously floats. Lily suffers from the paralysis of inertia. It is not that she is unaware of the void that gapes before her; it is rather that she has too much delicacy and sensitivity, that she is too much of a lady to make the kind of marriage that will save her from the fate of turning gradually from a guest into a hanger-on. Her father has been of old New York, but her mother, one gathers, is of more ordinary material, and it has been the latter's greed that has driven him to make the fortune that he is bound, by the same web of fate that enmeshes his daughter, to lose. So Lily is of both worlds; she understands both, and, before she has done, she has slipped between them and fallen prostrate beneath their stamping feet. The pathos of her fall is that the failure to act which precipitates each stage of her descent does not come from any superiority of moral resolution but rather from a refinement of taste, a fastidiousness, of which neither her meticulous aunt, Mrs. Peniston, nor her coarse admirer, Mr. Rosedale, have the remotest understanding. Indeed, one feels that Lily Bart, in all New York, is the lone and solitary lady. Yet with each slip in the ladder she experiences the coarsening that comes with the increased sense of the necessity of holding on, and though she can never bring herself to tell George Dorset of his wife's infidelity, even to win the town's richest husband and triumph over her most vindictive opponent, she can ultimately face the prospect of marriage with Sim Rosedale as a way of getting the money to pay a debt of honor. And when she does stoop it is too late; even Sim Rosedale won't have her, and Lily takes the final drop to the milliner's shop and ultimately to the overdose of sleeping tablets.

In *The Custom of the Country* Mrs. Wharton is again dealing with the conflict of materialisms, but this time the central study is of a parvenu, Undine Spragg, who cuts her way to the top of the heap. Her victim — for there is always a victim — is a man. Ralph Marvell is self-consciously of "aboriginal New York"; his forebears whose tradition he can never forget have been "small, cautious, middle-class" in their ideals, with "a tranquil disdain for money-getting" and "a passive openness to the finer sensations." But Ralph has just enough curiosity to be interested in "the invaders," as he calls the new rich; with cultivated decadence he finds an essential simplicity in their acquisitiveness. His cousin, Clare, another victim, has married invader Peter Van Degen and learned to repent, "but she repented in the Van Degen diamonds, and the Van Degen motor bore her broken heart from opera to ball." Ralph sees it all clearly, but he is to be different. He is to save the "innocence" of the Spraggs; he is to keep *them* from corruption. He goes down to speedy ruin before Undine, and his suicide is almost a matter of course. The victim, however, is too naïve; one's sympathy is confounded with impatience. It is Undine's book; her victims are incidental. She is the personification of the newcomer, absolutely vulgar and absolutely ruthless. Everything happens to Undine, but nothing affects her. She marries once for money, a second time for family and a third time for money again, only to find in the end that her divorces will keep her from being an ambassadress. And that, of course, is the only thing that she ultimately wants.

The Custom of the Country appeared in 1913, and the next four years Mrs. Wharton devoted entirely to war work. Her main job was with the Red Cross in Paris, but she visited military hospitals at the front and from a cottage garden at Clermont-en-Argonne she witnessed the victorious French assault on the heights of Vauquois. But the "fantastic heights and depths of self-devotion and ardor, of pessimism, triviality and selfishness," as she describes the war years, did little more for her as a writer than they have done, in either war, for many others. Their most important effect was to introduce a note of nostalgia, an escape, as she describes it, to childhood memories of a long-vanished America, to the "mild blur of rosy and white-whiskered gentlemen, of ladies with bare sloping shoulders rising flower-like from voluminous skirts, peeped at from the stair-top while wraps were removed in the hall below." But this was the New York, was it not, that she had found so stuffy and confining, that she had shown in losing battle with the Spraggs and Rosedales and from which she had fled to Europe? It was a New York, was it not, that had been passive, inert, confining, a city that had almost deserved to be eaten up by the new money of the energetic parvenu? Now, however, that it was gone, really gone, she found herself looking about and wondering if she had not gone too far in its condemnation. Much later she was to confess:

> When I was young it used to seem to me that the group in which I grew up was like an empty vessel into which no new wine would ever again be poured. Now I see that one of its uses lay in preserving a few drops of an old vintage too rare to be savored by a youthful palate.

Out of this sense of apology came *The Age of Innocence*. It deals with a New York that is pre-Spragg and pre-Rosedale. Newbold Archer is the young Whartonian of brownstone lineage, the Marvell type, a lawyer, of course, with a leisurely practice and an eye for books and pictures. He marries conventionally, and the story of the book is that he does *not* leave his wife to go off with the Countess Olenska, New York born but emancipated. There is no feeling, however, that Archer has condemned himself and the Countess to an unrewarding life of frustration. The author is absorbed in the beauty of rules and forms even when they stamp out spontaneity. "It was you," the Countess tells Archer, "who made me understand that under the dullness there are things so fine and sensitive and delicate that even those I most cared for in my other life look cheap in comparison." This is the climax of the message: that under the thick glass of convention blooms the fine, fragile flower of patient suffering and denial. To drop out of society is as vulgar as to predominate; one must endure and properly smile.

The novel, however, despite its note of calm resignation and sacrifice, is pervaded with a sense of materialism. The presence of "things" clogs even the best of Mrs. Wharton's writing. The author of *The House of Mirth* was also the author of *The Decoration of Houses.* One feels the charm of Ellen Olenska, but one feels it too much in her taste and possessions: "some small slender tables of dark wood, a delicate little Greek bronze in the chimney piece, and a stretch of red damask nailed on the discolored wallpaper behind a couple of Italian-looking pictures in old frames." She has "only two" Jacqueminot roses in a slender vase, and her tea is served "with handleless Japanese cups and little covered dishes." She finds a friend in Philistia; he understands Europe, and their refuge is in the arts, but their talk is filled with references to private rooms at Delmonico's and "little oyster suppers." Even in her moment of greatest emotional strain, when she looks at her watch she looks at a "little gold-faced watch on an enameled chain." The vigor of the earlier books is largely gone, but the sense of the world remains.

It was now that Edith Wharton found herself at the

crossroads. She could have continued in the nostalgic vein of *The Age of Innocence* and tethered herself, in James's phrase, to the native pastures of her early memories. The tendency might have been toward the sentimental, but the result could have had the charm of remembered things. One can see this in the little series known as *Old New York.* But, unfortunately, she chose for her major efforts the contemporary scene, especially the American scene, although it was a decade since she had crossed the Atlantic to revisit her native shores. Older and shriller, she denounced the vulgarity that she was now beginning to find in everything, judging America, the country in her eyes most responsible, by the standards of Riviera expatriates whom she did not even know.

The vulgarity on which she had declared war ended by overwhelming her novels. Taste, the chosen guide of her later years, went back on her. In the final dissolution, as with the Barts and Rosedales, conflict is again lost in merger. The very titles of the later books betray the drop of her standards; they are flat and ugly: *Human Nature, The Mother's Recompense*, *Twilight Sleep*, *The Glimpses of the Moon.* The caricature of American life becomes grotesque. The towns are given names like Delos, Aeschylus, Lohengrin or Halleluja, and the characters speak an anglicized dialect full of such terms as "Hang it!", "Chuck it!", "He's a jolly chap" and "A fellow needs . . ." The town slogan of Euphoria in *Hudson*

River Bracketed is "Me for the front row." And the American face! How it haunts her! It is "as unexpressive as a football"; it might have been made by "a manufacturer of sporting goods." Its sameness encompasses her "with its innocent uniformity." How many of such faces would it take "to make up a single individuality"? And, ironically enough, as her indignation mounts her style loses its old precision and begins to take on the slickness of a popular magazine story. Compare, for example, these two descriptions of a lady on the threshold of a European hotel. The first is from *Madame de Treymes*, written in 1907, one of her Jamesian passages, but highly polished:

> The mere fact of her having forgotten to draw on her gloves as they were descending in the hotel lift from his mother's drawing room was, in this connection, charged with significance to Durham. She was the kind of woman who always presents herself to the mind's eye as completely equipped, as made of exquisitely cared for and finely related details; and that the heat of her parting with his family should have left her unconscious that she was emerging gloveless into Paris seemed, on the whole, to speak hopefully for Durham's future opinion of the city. Even now, he could detect a certain confusion, a desire to draw breath and catch up with her life, in the way she dawdled over the last but-

tons in the dimness of the porte-cochère, while her footman, outside, hung on her retarded signal.

The second is from *The Glimpses of the Moon*, fifteen years later:

> But on the threshold a still more familiar figure met her: that of a lady in exaggerated pearls and sables, descending from an exaggerated motor, like the motors in magazine advertisements, the huge arks in which jeweled beauties and slender youths pause to gaze at snow peaks from an Alpine summit.

Specimens of old New York in the novels now become spindly and ridiculous, like Mr. Wyant in *Twilight Sleep* and Mr. Spears in *Hudson River Bracketed.* The Wheaters in *The Children* are meant to be rich New Yorkers traveling in Europe. Their children, of various nationalities, their absurd marital mix-up, their impossible, red-carpeted, be-yachted life, with a movie star ex-wife whose favorite swear word is "Fudge!" and an American-born princess who hopes that the size of families will be regulated by legislation, constitute a grotesque parody of international drifters. Mrs. Wharton has no true insight into their lives; she stands apart like her spokesman, Mrs. Sellars, in disdain, describing the Wheaters only in terms of snobbish and disapproving suppositions.

Eventually there seemed to be no aspect of American

life that did not disgust her. It was not only the vulgar rich; there were also the vulgar intellectuals. This passage from *The Gods Arrive* is meant to represent a conversation between young American writers in Paris:

> "Poor old Fynes," another of them took it up, "sounded as if he'd struck a new note because he made his people talk in the vernacular. Nothing else new about *him* — might have worked up his method out of Zola. Probably did."
>
> "Zola — who's he?" somebody yawned.
>
> "Oh, I dunno. The French Thackeray, I guess."
>
> "See here, fellows, who's read Thackeray, anyhow?"
>
> "Nobody since Lytton Strachey, I guess."
>
> "Well, anyway, 'This Globe' is one great big book. Eh, Vance, that the way you see it?"
>
> Vance roused himself and looked at the speaker. "Not the way I see life. Life's continuous!"
>
> "Life continuous — continuous? Why, it's a series of jumps in the dark. That's Mendel's law, anyhow," another budding critic took up the argument.
>
> "Gee! Who's Mendel? Another new novelist?"

The meeting between Mrs. Wharton and Scott Fitzgerald, as described by Arthur Mizener, is symptomatic of her uneasy relationships with the younger generation of writers. She found him crude, and he found her stiff and superior. But behind his sophomoric urge to shock a strait-laced old lady, lurked intense admiration and curiosity. He confessed once, half seriously, to Margaret Chanler that he had three ambitions in life: to write the best and clearest prose of the twentieth century, to remain faithful to Zelda and to become an intimate friend of Mrs. Wharton. Mrs. Chanler's response was the same that her friend Edith might have made: "As to your first ambition, I hope you attain it. As to your second, it is too personal for me to comment on. But as to your third, young man, you'll have to cut down your drinking!"

As with so many who seem proud and stiff, Mrs. Wharton's real trouble lay in shyness. She described it to Adèle Burden as the "dread disease" that had martyrized her in youth. She had finally come to terms with the world of her contemporaries, and it may have seemed too much to have to fight that battle with a new generation. She resented the formlessness of a world that seemed to have repudiated the very formalities that she had once satirized. When *The Mother's Recompense* was misunderstood by critics, she was deeply discouraged by the "densities of comprehension" that surrounded her. She wrote to Mrs. Chanler:

> You will wonder that the priestess of the life of reason should take such things to heart, and I wonder too. I never have minded before, but as my work reaches its close, I feel so sure that it is either

nothing, or far more than they know. And I wonder, a little desolately, which?

In 1937, the year in which she died, Mrs. Wharton was working on a novel that shows a brief, renewed interest in the New York of her childhood from which she drew *The Age of Innocence.* This is the posthumously published fragment, *The Buccaneers*, the unfinished story of three American girls in the seventies who make brilliant English marriages and become the envy of a New York which had scorned them. The book has more life than its immediate predecessors, but on its very opening page we find its author still laying on satire at the expense of America with the now customary trowel. She refers to certain tall white columns on the portico of the Grand Union Hotel in Saratoga which "so often reminded cultured travelers of the Parthenon at Athens (Greece)."

Guy Thwarte in this unfinished tale is the thread that links it with so many of its predecessors. Although English, he is still the Wharton hero, tall and good-looking, a Gibson man, and, to the amazement of his family, though he has a "decent reputation about women" and is a "brilliant point-to-point rider," he "messes about" with poetry and painting. Like the heroes of French classic tragedy the Wharton men keep their action off stage. Guy consents to dip into commerce, but only in foreign climes. He disappears to Brazil for four years and returns a millionaire, but the "dark, rich stormy years of his exile" lie "like a raging channel between himself and his old life." The notes at the end of the book show that he was fated to elope with the Duchess of Tintagel; it was to be the triumph of "love, deep and abiding love." One cannot feel after this any keen regret that the story was never finished. Lily Bart's love for Lawrence Selden is the one hollow note of *The House of Mirth*. Undine Spragg in *The Custom of the Country* is, of course, incapable of love. Love in *The Age of Innocence* is stifled by the characters themselves. Mrs. Wharton at her best was an analyst of the paralysis that attends failure in the market place and of the coarseness that attends success. Hers was not a world where romance was apt to flourish.

The Two Ages of Thackeray

MY WIFE owns a pair of pink vases which came from her great-grandmother's house in Lenox and which are decorated with medallion portraits of those unhappy friends, Marie-Antoinette and Madame de Lamballe. The pink is soft and warm, and the vases are pleasing to contemplate, but one sees at a glance that they are engaged in the hopeless struggle of Victorian porcelain to evoke the elusive charm and grace of the eighteenth century. There is too much ormulu on their sides and covers, too many curves in their design, too much placidity in the features of the doomed princesses. They belong in a cluttered window on Madison Avenue amid gallants with powdered hair leaning over to kiss the hands of ladies stepping out of sedan chairs and cardinals taking snuff and all those other porcelain figures who mince and simper like amateurs in a performance of

The School for Scandal. The nineteenth century, torn between envy and disdain, could never grasp the subtlety of its predecessor. The Widow of Windsor had her qualities, but they were not those of the Pompadour.

Thackeray, like my wife's vases, belonged to the later, but hankered after the earlier age. The eighteenth was always his favorite century. He cultivated its relics, lectured on its humorists and kings, and used it as a setting for a considerable part of his fiction. He was a frequent caller on the ancient Berry sisters, who continued to use the old-fashioned rouge and pearl powder and to garnish their conversation with such oaths as "O Christ!" and "My God!" His novels are spotted with sour references to the false prudishness of his own time and its hampering effect on writers. "Since the author of *Tom Jones* was buried," he declares indignantly in his preface to *Pendennis*, "no writer of fiction among us has been permitted to depict to his utmost power a *Man*." And in *The Virginians* he delivers this passionate apostrophe to the shade of Richardson:

> Oh, my faithful, good old Samuel Richardson! Hath the news yet reached thee in Hades that thy sublime novels are huddled away in corners, and that our daughters may no more read *Clarissa* than *Tom Jones?* I wonder whether a century hence the novels of today will be hidden behind locks and wires and make pretty little maidens blush?

We can only hope that the news has not reached Thackeray in Hades that the novels of *his* day are too tepid for the pretty little maidens of 1960. Richardson might have predicted it, but never Thackeray. For the Victorian age blanketed Europe and America in a fog of fatuity so dense that it was almost impossible for anyone living in it to see his way out. Thackeray may have thought of himself as a denizen of the Age of Reason, but we think of him as a leading and rather characteristic Victorian. How it would have pained him!

Yet how can we imagine the rosy-cheeked Clive Newcome in any century but the nineteenth? Or good Amelia or patient Laura or "that touching and wonderful spectacle of innocence and love and beauty," Helen Pendennis? And doesn't the famous ending of *Esmond*, which is supposed to take place in the early days of George I, belong in spirit to the era of the Brontës?

> And then the tender matron, as beautiful in her autumn, and as pure as virgins in their spring, with blushes of love and "eyes of meek surrender" yielded to my respectful importunity and consented to share my home.

Nobody, of course, was more sentimental than Richardson, but there was a wide difference between the sentimentalities of the two centuries. It is impossible to imagine Amelia Sedley or Laura Pendennis or Rachel Esmond suffering the fate of Clarissa Harlowe. The purity of Thackeray's heroines acts as a sensitive antenna to give them early warning of danger. Laura Pendennis, for example, stirs uneasily in the presence of Lady Clara Newcome long before that unfortunate lady has even contemplated her guilty elopement. She would have smelled out Lovelace's evil intentions at their first meeting.

Where Thackeray, however, is by no means typically Victorian is in his distrust — sometimes it almost seems his dislike — of the ladies whose virtue he extols. When the faithful Dobbin finally wins Amelia, she bores him. He prefers their little daughter to the mother for whom he has waited so long. Rachel Esmond's incessant jealousy proves a trial to both her husbands, and Laura Pendennis, that saint of saints, causes Colonel Newcome's death by insisting on the reunion of Rosey and Clive, which subjects the old man to the withering conversational fire of the Old Campaigner. But Laura, like so many holy persons, never stops to consider the consequences of her good advice. She blindly follows her simple rules and blandly reaps havoc and destruction.

This chink in Thackeray's Victorian armor was promptly detected by Charlotte Brontë who appeared on the London horizon like a tiny, astigmatic avenging angel to herald the dawn of a triumphant moral seriousness. She combined the virtues of her era with its worst faults, and was surely the clumsiest craftsman ever to scale Parnassus. Her plots are melodramatic, her prose purple, her dialogues labored and sententious, her satire embarrassingly obvious and her narrators smug, censorious and sentimental. What is it that redeems *Jane Eyre* and *Villette?* The classic answer is passion, Jane's passion for Rochester and Lucy Snowe's passion for Paul Emanuel. But I submit it is not so. It is the vital if unlovable force of Charlotte Brontë's egocentricity that makes these novels so curiously interesting, as it is Queen Victoria's that fascinates us in her journals and letters. They had much in common, those two sober, dour little women of immense sentimentality, immense dignity and immense self-importance. That they took themselves so seriously induces us to take them with equal seriousness. We are engrossed in the story of Jane Eyre long before Mr. Rochester makes his appearance. The cruelty of Mrs. Reed and the evils of Lowood School are just as interesting as his projected bigamy. The reason that *Shirley* is unreadable is that no character directly represents the author. We are left in the wasteland of Charlotte's writing without the oasis of Charlotte herself.

Miss Brontë had placed Thackeray on a towering pedestal before she ever met him. She had even dedicated the second edition of *Jane Eyre* to him. But like so many Victorians she proved an aggressive disciple. She had to get up on the pedestal with a chisel to try to improve the image. When she came to know her hero, she was shocked to discover that he was an enthusiastic frequenter of the very society that he satirized so sharply.

A less earnest observer could have inferred as much from his style. I know, for example, that the author who describes Mrs. Rawdon Crawley's stylish little supper parties must have enjoyed their counterparts, just as I know that Proust loved dining at the Guermantes' and Ouida would have loved court balls, and just as I know that the woman who conceived that ghastly dinner party which Mr. Rochester gives for Blanche Ingraham must have had a deep and sincere loathing for all forms of social life. Miss Brontë had no use for greys; she liked her blacks to be black and her whites white. She marched in upon Thackeray, as he himself put it, like "an austere little Joan of Arc" to rebuke his easy life and easy morals. He found her amusing, if a bit trying, and liked to exasperate her, as when he introduced her to his mother as "Jane Eyre," despite her clinging to the veil of her pen name. But I have an idea that she stung him more than he cared to admit. "She was angry with her favorites," he says, "if their conduct or conversation fell below her ideal." It is always pleasing to one writer to be the passionate ideal of another. Miss Brontë's approbation, after all, was almost the approbation of their era, and her frowns were almost its frowns. The Victorian in Thackeray must have winced at the scorn of so pure a Victorian. He sent her the galley sheets of *Esmond*, and the first authority on his life and letters, Gordon Ray, believes that her exhortations may have borne fruit in the "nobler tone" of that novel.

As Thackeray grew older, he began to have his doubts about his beloved eighteenth century. True, to the end of his life, he maintained a literary attitude of being pro-Augustan and anti-prude (and Mr. Ray speaks of his fondness for dirty limericks), but one notices the increasing sternness with which he judges his predecessors, both fictional and real. In *The Virginians* Beatrix Esmond, now an old woman, who, for all her wickedness, is given the heavy task of enlivening a dull book, illuminates George Warrington on the history of the Castlewood family, using words "not used by ladies of a later time." "And so much the better on the whole," the author comments. "We mayn't be more virtuous, but it is something to be more decent. Perhaps we are not more pure, but of a surety we are more cleanly." Harry Warrington, in the same novel, is a healthy young man from the colonies who is dazzled by the fuss made over him by the London social world. He drinks and gambles and is seen in the company of a French actress of notorious reputation. Yet when jokes are made about her, Harry is ready to draw his sword. He believes in her virtue, as he believes in every woman's. Even conceding that the Victorian had to make concessions to the contemporary censor, surely he did not have to go this far. Harry and his brother, George, cease to be believable as young blades of their century. They are really ambassadors to the England of George II, not from Virginia, but from the Victorian age, legates across time and not space.

Ultimately, Thackeray turned even on such a former favorite as Fielding. Here is his famous verdict on Tom Jones:

> I can't say that I think Mr. Jones a virtuous character; I can't say but that I think Fielding's evident liking and admiration for Mr. Jones, shows that the great humorist's moral sense was blunted by his life, and that here in Art and Ethics, there is a great error.

On Sterne he is even more severe, and he ends his lecture on the author of *Tristram Shandy* with a tribute to Dickens that would seem to enroll him with such lofty Victorians as Martin Tupper and Lord Tennyson:

> There is not a page in Sterne's writing but has something that were better away, a latent corruption — a hint, as of an impure presence. . . . I think of these past writers and of one who lives amongst us now, and am grateful for the innocent laughter and the sweet and unsullied page which the author of *David Copperfield* gives to my children.

Towards the end of his life we find him, as editor of the *Cornhill Magazine*, rejecting Trollope's *Mrs. General Tallboys* because of allusions to illegitimate children and to a woman not as pure as she should be. Had Miss Brontë been living, she might have at last been satisfied.

But if Thackeray, as he grew older, became an increasingly complacent Victorian novelist, he became also the greatest of them. I can forgive the century a great deal of complacency that produced *The Newcomes.* It is less read today than *Vanity Fair* or *Esmond*, but the critics of Thackeray's time thought it his finest work. It is a verdict in which I fully concur, though it is not easy to explain why. The faults of *The Newcomes* loom large when considered together.

Surely the story is told in a loose and rambling fashion. Surely great chunks of it are boring. Does anyone care today about Clive Newcome's opinion of Italian painting? Or about the frolics of those young artists who caper as clumsily as Rudolfo's fellow tenants in the first act of *La Bohème?* Is it Thackeray's portrait of a family that gives the novel its peculiar excellence? Gordon Ray says that when we have finished, we know the Newcomes as no other family in fiction. But I question this. The first Mrs. Newcome is little more than a caricature. Her sons, Brian and Hobson, are lightly sketched, and their wives, Lady Ann and Maria, like Dickens characters, say the same things every time they appear. Lady Ann is always languid, and Maria, like Madame Verdurin in Proust, is always being scornful of the people whom she can't catch for her parties. Of the children of Hobson we learn almost nothing, and of the children of Brian we know only Barnes and Ethel. Of three generations, therefore, we have complete studies only of Colonel Newcome, his son Clive, his nephew Barnes, and his niece Ethel. It should also be noted that Thackeray utterly ignores family characteristics. Barnes and Ethel, although brother and sister, have nothing whatever in common, nor really, except for a similarity about pulling whiskers, do Clive and his father. As a matter of fact, I fail to see that any Newcome resembles any other Newcome.

Wherein, then, is the excellence? Well, of course, Colonel Newcome is a great character. We see him clearly, in all his innocence and foolishness and generosity. And we understand his relationship with Clive. Actually, the "Newcomes" boil down to the Colonel and Clive. If Ethel and Barnes belonged to a different family, I doubt that the book would lose much. I even suggest that the device of linking all the characters by means of a family tree is the author's artifice to create an illusion of unity. It allows him to run out on branches whenever he wishes without incurring the charge of evasiveness. In justice to Galsworthy, who has often been compared unfavorably with Thackeray, the Forsytes seem to me more a family than the Newcomes.

Take the novel, then, as the study of a father who adores, without ever understanding, his only son, and who ultimately destroys himself, and very nearly the son, in a valiant but misguided effort to buy the world and lay it at his boy's feet. Of course, there must be a girl who will be the one thing that the son wants and that the father cannot buy for him, and Ethel fulfills this role to perfection. And, of course, there must be a villain to ruin the old man, and Barnes is a perfect villain. Having reduced the plot to its essentials, suppose we then cut the novel to these four characters and their interrelationship. What do we lose? Simply half of Thackeray's effect. His art is far more than characterization.

But what is it? What is the "richness" that the critics speak of? Does it consist of his long asides, of his interminable lectures on morality, of his elaborate sketching of minor figures, of his evident anxiety to seize upon any distraction to avoid getting on with his story and to fill out the yellow-backed serials in which his novels appeared? Perhaps. There is some of the charm of a stage rehearsal or of visiting a sculptor in his studio in watching Thackeray at work. He appears to conceal nothing from our eyes, and all around lie the props of his art, beautiful backdrops, half-finished figures, chisels, hammers, odd piles of tarpaulin. But there in the center are his great creations: Becky Sharpe, Major Pendennis and above all, above everything, Colonel Newcome. We can never lose sight of them, nor does he. He is quite aware how good they are, and however much he talks or rants or chisels or hammers, he keeps drawing our attention back to them.

We begin to perceive, then, what it is that makes *The Newcomes* a great book. It is the combination of the sculptured figure and the sculptor. While we admire the finished product we find it agreeable to listen to the author. His personality surrounds his work without overwhelming it, like Charlotte Brontë's. Thackeray is an urbane nineteenth century guide and commentator in a portrait gallery that is for all time. One's guide, after all, must be of some era, and I would not have Thackeray in any other. I like him just as he is, the restless inhabitant of a prudish age, nostalgic, discursive, anecdotal, sentimental, worldly-wise, now warning us, now making fun of us, now reproving us. If he is Victorian, he is charmingly Victorian. One wonders, in the end, if he did not owe his greatest debt to the era he loved to deplore.

He owed the era one other debt, which I will mention by way of conclusion, and that is his reputation for cynicism. His name has become almost synonymous with cynicism, simply because his works are saturated with a creed of three basic tenets: (1) that everything yearned for is apt to be a disappointment when realized; (2) that London society is full of toadies, and (3) that the motivation behind acts of apparent altruism is usually self-interest. The last tenet is best summed up in a passage from *The Newcomes:*

> You are pleased that yesterday, at dinner, you refrained from the dry champagne? My name is Worldly Prudence, not Self-denial, and *I* caused you to refrain. You are pleased, because you gave a guinea to Diddler? I am Laziness, not Generosity,

which inspired you. You hug yourself because you resisted other temptation? Coward, it was because you dared not run the risk of wrong. Off with your peacock's plumage!

Imagine an author of today writing a novel to illustrate such tenets! Far from being called a cynic, he would be lucky not to find himself pilloried as a Pollyanna. For Thackeray's harshest criticism of humanity is simply the point where ours commences. His perception of self-interest in every act is the ABC of modern psychology. The whole machinery of our tax law reflects the assumption that every man will arrange his affairs to effect the maximum evasion of imposts. We see a yacht or a limousine or a large party at a restaurant, and consider ourselves simple realists, not cynics, when we shrug our shoulders and mutter "Tax deduction" or "Business expense." That a man should consider his economic welfare before the welfare of his nation is so taken for granted that we require our foremost citizens to liquidate their stockholdings before taking cabinet office. In sex, in family relations, in business, in politics, we calmly accept the brute force of the "id." Only in that curious Victorian era that seals off its decades from the rest of history in a kind of hothouse of willful illusion could Thackeray's gentle comments on the essential monkey in man have seemed unkind.

Is George Eliot Salvageable?

JAMES, in his uncompleted "The Middle Years," describes a visit to George Eliot and G. H. Lewes on a Sunday afternoon in the winter of 1878. He was taken by Mrs. Greville, that "large, elegant, extremely near-sighted and extremely demonstrative lady, whose genius was all for friendship, admiration, declamation and expenditure." The scene is highly comic, for the unhappy young novelist feels how little welcome is either he or his bustling companion in the austere parlor of the "bland, benign" author of *Romola.* The Leweses liked them to have come, but "mainly from a prevision of how they should more devoutly like it" when they departed. The nothingness of the visit is summed up in a single sentence:

> It is remarkable, but the occasion yields me no single echo of a remark on the part of any of us—

nothing more than the sense that our great author herself peculiarly suffered from the fury of the elements, and that they had about them rather the minimum of the paraphernalia of reading and writing, not to speak of that of tea, a conceivable feature of the hour, but which was not provided for.

When Lewes conducted the visitors to their carriage, "all sociably, *then* above all conversingly," he suddenly bethought himself of an item forgotten and hurried back into the house to secure a pair of blue-bound volumes that Mrs. Greville, on another occasion, had importunately loaned. As poor James received these from his hand and heard his "Ah those books — take them away, please away, away!" the title of his own precious "last" squinted up at him. Yet there was still a compensating Jamesian thrill, as he drove off with the mortified Mrs. Greville, "in thinking of persons — or at least of a person, for any fact about Lewes was but derivative — engaged in my own pursuit and yet detached, by what I conceived, detached by a pitch of intellectual life, from all that made it actual to myself."

Other observers were less charitable. Charles Eliot Norton, met at the door of the Priory by the accommodating Lewes, expected to see him "take up his fiddle and begin to play." The drawing room, hung with pictures of scenes from *Romola*, "bore witness to the want of delicate artistic feeling or good culture." As for his hostess, the Harvard professor had rarely seen a plainer woman, "dull complexion, dull eye, heavy features." She said "not one memorable thing in three hours," but behaved as "a woman who feels herself to be of mark and is accustomed, as she is, to the adoring flattery of a coterie of not undistinguished admirers."

"Always the goddess on her pedestal," was the sour comment of Eliza Lynn, a friend from obscurer days, "gracious in her condescension — with sweet strains of recognition."

The point of view of these observers ranges from enthusiasm to disgust, but the picture of the mournful priestess and her twittering major-domo remains a constant. The same atmosphere of solemn and faintly bogus self-importance hangs over the novels to repel the modern reader. I suppose it was not George Eliot's fault that her collected editions always contain, as well as those dreary, inevitable illustrations of rustic scenes in the Midlands, the famous portrait by Sir Frederick Burton which perpetuates the heavy features of which Norton spoke. But the trouble with George Eliot is that she *wanted* to look that way.

F. W. H. Myers, the author of *Human Personality and Its Survival of Bodily Death*, gives a description of her that reads like a caricature. Walking in Cambridge on an evening of rainy May, they discussed the words God, Immortality and Duty, and George Eliot pronounced with a terrible earnestness how inconceivable was the first, how unbelievable the second and yet how peremptory and absolute the third.

> Never perhaps have sterner accents affirmed the sovereignty of impersonal and unrecompensing Law. I listened, and night fell; her grave, majestic countenance turned towards me like a sibyl's in the gloom; it was as though she withdrew from my grasp, one by one, the two scrolls of promise and left me the third scroll only, awful with inevitable fates. And when we stood at length and parted, amid that columnar circuit of forest trees, beneath the last twilight of starlight skies, I seemed to be gazing, like Titus at Jerusalem, on vacant seats and empty halls — on a sanctuary with no presence to hallow it, and heaven left lonely of a God.

Yet the Victorian public must have liked views of vacant seats and empty halls, for George Eliot was the most popular serious writer of her day. She approached her task with the dedication of one taking an oath of high public office. "Man or woman who publishes writings," she warned the literary world, "inevitably assumes the office of teacher or influencer of the public mind." And supposing man or woman simply strives to be amusing? Supposing his only wish is to entertain? He becomes a distiller of "spiritual gin." The test is summed up:

> In endeavoring to estimate a writer one must ask: "Did he animate long-known but neglected truths with new vigour and cast fresh light on their relation to other admitted truths? Did he impregnate any ideas with a fresh store of emotion, and in this way enlarge the area of moral sentiment?"

But even in the heyday of her popularity some readers were beginning to stir resentfully at this conversion of a means of entertainment into a pulpit. Was the novel to be turned into a tract for the expounding of austere doctrine? James, in the same chapter where he records the unhappy visit with Mrs. Greville, notes the rise of this criticism:

> It was the fashion among the profane in short either to misdoubt, before George Eliot's canvas, the latter's backing of rich thought, or else to hold that this matter of philosophy . . . thrust itself through to the confounding of the picture. But with that thin criticism I wasn't . . . to have a moment's patience . . . I found the figured, coloured tapestry *always* vivid enough to brave no matter what complication of the stitch.

There is some of the enthusiasm of a generous colleague's final summation in this. Actually, James had not always found the tapestry quite so vivid, as an early review of *Felix Holt* can witness. It may be only sensible in looking at tapestries to concentrate on the figured, colored sections, but to a generation that wonders if there *are* any, one must first learn to avoid the areas of overcomplicated stitch. The question will be whether any of the tapestry is left.

Certainly the desolation that Myers felt in George Eliot's philosophy is the same that pervades her fiction. She was woefully preoccupied with duty. And it was duty, too, with no prospect of reward, or even approval, in this life or in any other, duty with no object other than that of the gradual amelioration of the lot of mankind. As the novels progress, this concept of duty becomes drearier and drearier, until it is ultimately duty for duty's sake, and we turn from it with a shudder of repulsion, as from something deformed.

Dinah Morris in *Adam Bede*, an early heroine, is the last to derive any pleasure out of doing her duty, but her duty is preaching, and who would not rather deliver that evangelical sermon on the village green than have to listen to it? Besides, Dinah has the impersonality of a saint; she loves mankind rather than men, which is why we are not convinced of her passion for Adam. Very likely Dinahs exist — I disagree with those who claim that she is altogether a wooden character — but they are no more interesting to meet than to read about. Maggie Tulliver in *The Mill on the Floss* is more sympathetic, and were it not for her habit of prosy moralizing we might become fond of her. But how much fondness can we feel for a girl who speaks in this fashion to her lover:

> We can only choose whether we will indulge ourselves in the present moment, or whether we will renounce that, for the sake of obeying the divine voice within us — for the sake of being true to all the motives that sanctify our lives.

Maggie's choice represents the Eliot sense of duty at its purest. She is not engaged to Philip Wakem, nor is Stephen Guest engaged to Lucy Dean. If she and Stephen marry, no pledge will be broken. On the other hand, Philip and Lucy will have nothing to gain from their renunciation, for the passion between Maggie and Stephen is too intense to allow either to fall back on a loveless match. Maggie is helped in her choice by the fact that the road of inclination is shaded by riches and social position, whereas the road of duty lies under the baking sun of poverty and disgrace. Obviously, then, duty must prevail; it makes for a perfect ending that Maggie will have nothing. As she tells Stephen:

> You feel, as I do, that the real tie lies in the feelings and expectations we have raised in other minds. Else all pledges might be broken, when there was no outward penalty. There would be no such thing as faithfulness.

And so, because Stephen has given Lucy grounds to expect a proposal, everyone's life must be ruined. Small wonder that George Eliot warned us to take the smallest things in life seriously. It was hardly safe for a young man to go to a party if he was to be bound forever by the "feelings and expectations" that he might raise in other minds. Can young people today, or could they in the last half century, for that matter, have any sympathy with such a theme? Gaillard Lapsley, who was Edith Wharton's literary executor, once told me that he could not imagine young people of my day caring for *The House of Mirth*, where Lily Bart's reputation is ruined simply because she is seen to emerge from the Trenors' house on a night when Mrs. Trenor is out of town. But it seemed to me that what saved the novel for modern readers was that Edith Wharton did not believe in the code under which Lily was condemned, and, indeed, there has been a big enough continuing public for *The House of Mirth* to justify its recent republication. What made George Eliot popular in her own day is precisely what has created her present neglect: she shares with the Victorian public an admiration for what we consider pointless sacrifice.

One of the oddest elements in the odd pastiche that is *Romola* is the anachronism of the Victorian goddess of duty in fifteenth century Florence. When the reader is not being dragged about the streets and piazzas to be exposed to the last drop of local color falling from the sternly wrung and rewrung washrag of George Eliot's research, he is made to sit and swallow great doses of moralizing. It was probably Savonarola who attracted her to this period of Italian history. She concedes that fanaticism may have ultimately carried him too far, but her basic admiration is conveyed through the medium of her heroine. At the burning of the pyramid of vanities on the Piazza della Signoria, on which the Florentines tossed not only their wigs and rouge pots, but their books of pagan authors and works of art, Romola is "conscious of no inward collision with the strict and sombre view of pleasure which tended to repress poetry in the attempt to repress vice." Her life has given her "an affinity for sadness which inevitably made her unjust towards merriment." But it is hardly an injustice that the author expects us to condemn. Romola, like Dinah, is a saint.

But whence her affinity for sadness? It comes, like that of other Eliot heroines, from their Achilles' heel of a violent sensibility. There is something pathetic but rather comic about these strong, noble, high-minded women who take fire at first sight of a handsome man. Surely, they are unreasonable in their bitterness at the ensuing disillusionment. By what right, having selected a mate by purely physical standards, do they expect to find a soul as beautiful as the outward form? Yet Romola has no tolerance of the least fault in her husband. She leaves him, not for his real crimes, of which she is still ignorant, but because he has sold her father's library. She then has a typically Eliot argument on the road with Savonarola. Between two duties, that of tending the poor and sick, and that of returning to her husband, Savonarola easily induces her to choose the second, being the more repugnant to her. There are compensations for Romola in the gratitude and veneration of the destitute about which her creator is surprisingly candid:

> "Bless you, Madonna! bless you!" said the faint chorus, in much the same tone as that in which they had a few minutes before praised and thanked the unseen Madonna. Romola cared a great deal for that music.

I would nominate Felix Holt for the most unlovable hero of Victorian fiction. In his very first words he announces his priggishness. The old minister, Rufus Lyon, explains to his guest, perhaps superfluously, that he uses wax light because his delicately framed daughter dislikes the smell of tallow. In "loud, abrupt tones" Holt replies:

> I heeded not the candle, sir. I thank Heaven I am not a mouse to have a nose that takes note of wax or tallow.

And in loud, abrupt tones he continues throughout the novel to catch everyone up on their slightest utterances until we join heartily with the judge and jury who condemn him to four years' imprisonment for a crime of which he is innocent. The other characters, however, join to get him off, though why they bother I cannot imagine, as in the best Eliot tradition he is perfectly willing to be locked up and has indulged himself in a rude speech to the court which seems designed to secure his conviction.

In *Daniel Deronda* the reader is allowed to enjoy himself for almost a third of the book before the duty figure appears to spoil his fun. But we know all the time that he is coming, for we have had a preparatory glimpse of his disapproving countenance at the gambling hall in the first chapter. Daniel Deronda is less offensive than Felix Holt because he is a silent rather than a noisy bore. But he is still offensive. He exudes disapproval of everybody, including the Jews, until he finds that he is one of them. Mirah regards him as her savior, though he has done little more than put her up at a friend's house, and Gwendolen looks upon him as a touchstone against the evil within herself, though his services consist only of little homilies whispered at dinner parties. But they both know he must be good because he is so gloomy.

If the performance of duty is a cheerless task, however, unlit by the prospect of reward or even of gratitude, there is at least the consolation, in Eliot novels, of considering the hideous fate of the undutiful. There may be no heaven, but there is certainly a hell, and right here on earth. Doom hangs over the characters and manifests itself in omens and sudden prognostications: the noise of a rat suggests the tap of a willow wand on the eve of old Bede's death; Dinah foresees Hetty's miserable destiny, and Mrs. Tulliver has a terror from the beginning that Maggie will get herself "drownded." Life is ready with knives and ropes to wreak its vengeance on the trivial-minded and the selfish. Gwendolen Harleth, Tito Melema and Hetty Sorel pay for their egotism with a ghastly price. Yet the reader cannot but feel that there should be a mitigation of the penalty because they, at least, have tried to entertain him.

The pity of it! That a writer with the power of characterization of a Thackeray, the narrative skill of a Trollope, the satirical eye of a Jane Austen and the descriptive ease of a Scott, should have wrecked her work with a foolish didacticism! Never have greater gifts been less valued by their owner. Imagine the perversity of the woman who could so enthrallingly describe the seduction of Hetty Sorel forcing our attention from that to the homilies of Dinah Morris! Imagine, after having started a story as brilliantly as she did *Felix Holt*, with the proud, bitter, disillusioned Mrs. Transome, ruining it with her prig of a hero! And imagine, after fixing our absorbed gaze on Gwendolen Harleth and her terrible marriage, sticking Daniel Deronda before our eyes! She seems to take a malicious pleasure in ringing down the curtain just when we are beginning to enjoy ourselves. "I turn," she says in *Adam Bede*, "without shrinking, from cloud-borne angels, from prophets, sibyls and heroic warriors, to an old woman bending over her flower pot, or eating her solitary dinner." She wanted her rustic novels to be like Dutch paintings, faithful pictures of a monotonous, homely existence. If that involved a loss of excitement and color, well, that was simply too bad:

> In writing the history of unfashionable families, one is apt to fall into a tone of emphasis which is very far from being the tone of good society, where principles and beliefs are not only of an extremely moderate kind, but are always presupposed, no subjects being eligible but such as can be touched with a light and graceful irony.

And this from a woman who was a mistress of irony! Who could say of Mrs. Glegg that, with a front and back parlor, she had "two points of view from which she could observe the weakness of her fellow-beings," and of Mr. Casaubon that "he determined to abandon himself to the stream of feeling and perhaps was surprised to find what an exceedingly shallow rill it was"! Are not Maggie Tulliver's aunts the literary ancestresses of Dorothy Parker's Mrs. Matson and Mrs. Whittaker?

What, then, is to be done about her? Can one expect the modern reader to work his way through *Adam Bede* for the sake of Hetty Sorel, or *The Mill on the Floss* for the Dodson sisters, or *Daniel Deronda* for Gwendolen and Grandcourt, or *Felix Holt* for Mrs. Transome? Can one even urge him to? I fear not. In poetry and music one can save choice bits from tedious works, but a novel is like a painting and can't be cut up, except for those vast anthologies of prose which one never sees again after freshman year.

Is anything left, then, except *Silas Marner* for high school students? Yes. *Middlemarch* is left. That may not, at first blush, seem much, but to me it is like saying that *Anna Karenina* is left. It is the fashion today for East and West to vie with each other in every field, and in an exhibition of nineteenth century fiction, I would offer *Middlemarch* against anything that the Russians could produce. How did it happen that George Eliot, after two dreary years of work on *Romola*, which she said had turned her into an old woman, and more on *Felix Holt* and much lamentable poetry, should suddenly have produced the greatest English novel of manners of the century? I think I can show that it was simply good luck.

It was a habit of Victorian writers to keep two or three plots running in parallel lines through a single novel, sometimes not tying them together until a melodramatic final chapter. We know that George Eliot sometimes conceived her individual plots quite independently of their future companions or even of the novel where they would ultimately meet. For example, there is evidence that she started work on the story of Dorothea Brooke and Mr. Casaubon long before the Garths or the Vincys or the town of Middlemarch itself had occurred to her. When she matched up her plots into novels, she was careful to give each entertaining one a sober and moralizing counterpart; we pay for Arthur Donnithorne with the Bede brothers and for Aunt Glegg and Aunt Pullet with Maggie. But in putting *Romola* together she forgot the entertainment, and in *Middlemarch*, by a happy fortune, she forgot the sermon. I like to speculate that one could create another *Middlemarch* out of existing Eliot fiction simply by a judicious use of scissors and paste. I would lift Hetty Sorel and Arthur out of *Adam Bede* and fit them into *Daniel Deronda* in the vacant spaces left by the excision of the hero and his plans for a Jewish state. They would thus provide an admirable contrast to Gwendolen and Grandcourt, illustrating the dangers of too little and of too much calculation in love. Arthur might even marry Gwendolen in the end. And I would bring Mrs. Transome over from *Felix Holt* to act as Grandcourt's mother and the Dodson sisters from *The Mill on the Floss* to be Hetty's aunts. The fascinating thing is how little one would violate any of George Eliot's conceptions. Her tragedy as a writer is that she never learned the simple lesson that an entertainer must entertain.

Dorothea Brooke, in *Middlemarch*, has all the nobility of soul of Maggie or Romola, but she is saved from being a bore by being a goose. I know of nothing better in English fiction than her deliberate, pathetic, perverted and entirely understandable impulse to throw herself away on the dried-up old scholar, Casaubon, and nothing better than his utter failure to appreciate either her character or her self-sacrifice. Critics of George Eliot's time were inclined to deplore Dorothea's passion for Ladislaw, as they were inclined to deplore Maggie's for Stephen Guest. They felt that such heroines should look higher. But what they failed to perceive was that Dorothea is never going to be ready for love until she has first realized the desperate folly of her marriage, and that then she will be ready to adore the first young man who looks kindly at her. There is a marvellous psychological moment when Dorothea, hearing that Mr. Casaubon has expressly provided in his will that a marriage to Ladislaw will cut off her income, feels a sudden rush of warmth towards the young man so prohibited to her. For until that moment nobody, including herself, has dared to articulate even the possibility of a romantic relationship between them. It is Casaubon's testamentary trick that, ironically enough, brings them together.

The situation of Rosamond Vincy and Lydgate is only a fraction less interesting: the helplessness of a brilliant man in the hands of a determined, mediocre woman. But Mary Garth is responsible for a slight drop in our attention because she has been so unfortunate as to incur the approbation of the author. As Gerald

Bullett points out, the chief thing an Eliot character has to fear is the unqualified moral approval of his creator. In Mary's first appearance, and later, in her father's, we feel the gathering of the grey clouds of that unmistakable Eliot dullness, but, happily, their role in the story is limited, and neither can do a "Deronda" to it.

Another habit of Victorian novelists, besides the weaving of multiple plots, was a "what happened after" piece by way of conclusion. The last chapter of *Middlemarch* has more to say in this respect than many others because it offers us a glimpse of Rosamond Vincy without which our understanding of her would not be complete. We learn that Lydgate dies at fifty, and that she marries an elderly and wealthy physician who took kindly to her four children. "She made a very pretty show with her daughters, driving out in her carriage, and often spoke of her happiness as 'a reward.' " Lydgate has rightly called her the basil plant that feeds on the brains of murdered men. To me there is a greater enlargement of the "area of moral sentiment" in this picture of the triumph of a stubborn female mediocrity over male genius and imagination than in all of Gwendolen Harleth's frantic soul searching in snatched moments at parties with the embarrassed and cliché-loving Deronda. But I doubt if George Eliot would have agreed with me. She had a fatal fondness for underscoring her points.

The Little Duke and the Great King

SAINT-SIMON AND LOUIS XIV

I AM ALWAYS a bit surprised, whenever I turn back to the memoirs of the Duc de Saint-Simon, at the classic judgment of the French court as a shrine of artificiality and hypocrisy. Every beginner of French history knows the quotation from Taine's courtier: "A genuine sentiment is so rare that, when I leave Versailles, I sometimes stand still in the street to see a dog gnaw a bone." I can see, of course, that life in a crowded palace may have had some of the artificiality of life in a zoo, but that does not have to mean that the courtiers, any more than the animals, *behaved* artificially in it. And as for hypocrisy, would that Saint-Simon had more of it to describe! Except for the fawning over Louis XIV, some of which was perfectly sincere (the king, after all, *was* the state), the people in the memoirs behave with a brutal frankness and a doglike rapacity that is appalling to behold

Was somebody dying? The talk was only of who would succeed to his offices. To shed a tear was to be accused of the grossest insincerity. Family relationships that we regard as the most vital things in life acted as little or no brake to the march of self-interest. Parents and children regarded each other with a detachment, the example of which was set by their sovereign, who, when the Duchesse de Bourgogne suffered a miscarriage, simply observed:

> Has she not a son already? And if he died, is not the Duc de Berri of an age to marry and have children? What do I care which of them succeeds me? Are they not equally my grandchildren? Since she was to have a miscarriage, thank God it is over! I shall no longer be bothered and hampered in everything I want to do by the remonstrances of doctors and matrons.

I am quite aware of Madame de Sévigné and her idolatry of her daughter, but her death is recorded early in the memoirs. Her era was pre-Versailles. Madame de Grignan, whose filial coolness can be read between the lines of her mother's impassioned letters, was more of Saint-Simon's age. Self-indulgence was carried into everything, from love to personal habits. Dogs, surely, could hardly have yielded with more freedom to sexual impulses than the denizens of Versailles, and their lack of inhibition in other matters was commented on with disgust by foreign observers. We even read of one lady who left a "filthy trail" behind her when she got up from the dinner table. The young people occupied their leisure time with hazing and practical jokes such as the following:

> Another time, also at Marly, there had been a heavy fall of snow, and it was freezing hard. The Duchesse de Bourgogne and her suite armed themselves with a quantity of snowballs, slipped quietly into the bedroom of the Princesse d'Harcourt, drew back her curtains suddenly, and overwhelmed her with a shower of snowballs. The sight of this dirty creature in bed, suddenly awakened, dishevelled, shrieking at the top of her voice and wriggling like an eel, amused them for nearly half an hour; but it was almost enough to kill her.

Yet it was this same Duchesse de Bourgogne who "tried to make everybody love her, even the most insignificant and apparently useless people"! One wonders if the impromptu royal visit with the snowballs was intended as a means of access to the heart of Madame d'Harcourt. After only a few chapters of Saint-Simon I find myself giving prayerful thanks that we have outgrown the "naturalness" of the French court. Who would not prefer a little harmless hypocrisy?

But is it true? Were they that bad? It seems quite possible. Take several thousand persons and squash them into a palace so densely that the greatest duke may have only three small, smelly rooms, and you create a kind of gilded Dotheboys Hall, where adults will regress into a ferocious childhood. The men will fight for honors as schoolboys for medals. They will have nothing to think about but their own position vis-a-vis the others, and how can that be indicated except by tags? I shall keep reverting to the analogy of the school, because it seems to me the key to the puzzle of Versailles. It was a school, except there were no diplomas. Louis XIV did not allow anyone to graduate.

Saint-Simon is the perfect guide to the era because his philosophy is almost a parody of the prevailing philosophy. He believed that all history could be boiled down to the simple question of precedence. A good man was one who knew his rung on the ladder and remained perched on it. A great man was one who saw to it that everyone else remained perched on theirs. A bad man was one who tried to climb to a higher rung, and a weak man was one who allowed a bad man to climb over him. Any movement on the ladder, up or down, tended to shake the civilized order. At times Saint-Simon carries it so far that he seems more of a caricaturist than a historian. All of France, all of Europe, is lit up against the ludicrous backdrop of the social ladder. Coaches clash in narrow streets because their owners refuse to yield the right of way; duchesses scuffle and elbow each other for position at the king's table. Foreign princes are entertained out of doors, even in inclement weather, to avoid questions as to the order of passing into a house, and hosts, feigning illness, are carried into dining rooms in litters, to sup lying down, that it may not be said that they have made way for guests of honor. Behind every human act or omission to act the sharp eye of the memoirist detects the eternal question of rank.

He may, of course, have exaggerated. He had a widespread reputation in his own day for disputatiousness in questions of etiquette which he blandly assumed to be a mark of the world's esteem. And we can see in his own self-portrait the jealous eye, the explosive temper and the shrill boldness of the man who is quick to find a personal slight in the least inadvertence. But we learn about disease by the study of desperate cases, and Saint-Simon is an example of how sick the nobility was. In his private audiences with the king we observe the relationship of the squirrel and the mountain. The former can crack a nut, the nut of his perpetual grievances, but it is about all he can do. Perhaps Louis XIV managed to contain his patience by reminding himself that giving ear to the complaints of his courtiers was part of his system. To keep an eye on his squirrels, he had to keep them at court. And so long as he kept an eye on them, they could never become anything but squirrels.

Louis XIV was the perfect monarch — according to the system which he himself had devised. It was to serve as a model to the crowned heads of Europe for the next century, and one of its numerous faults was that its founder was the only person capable of living up to it. It provided, in brief, that the king should be the splendid living symbol of the state every minute of his waking hours, that he should perform every function, including his bodily ones, in public, that he should comport himself at all times with stately good manners and majestic mien, that he should have no intimates even in his family (his morganatic wife complained that he had "no conversation"), that he should permit no liberties and that his court, his palaces, his very gardens should be magnificent extensions of himself, always on parade, always in full dress, both in times of prosperity and in days of darkest depression. To accomplish this end, the sovereign had to have an implacable will power, a complete absence of humor and a robust constitution. Louis XIV qualified in all three respects. In addition, having succeeded his father at the age of four, he could not remember a time when he had not been king. But he remembered vividly and bitterly the civil wars of his minority and their hideous affront to his dignity, and his simple, implacable, lifelong revenge was the slow emasculation of the peerage, enmeshed in the endless ceremonial of the Versailles court. What an assuagement it must have been to the persistent anxiety engendered in his childhood by impudent *frondeurs* to look out over that sea of bowing heads to fountains and canals that carried his glory to the horizon!

Yet it was a backbreaking job. Later monarchs, exhausted by his system, created Petits Trianons to get away from it. Louis XIV never got away. When he went to Marly or Fontainebleau he took as much of his court with him as those smaller residences would contain. And he always had to know who was at court and who was away and who had died and who wanted what. He could not afford to despise the subjects of the petty disputes that sterilized the power of his dukes. He might keep the peers out of his cabinet, but he had to be careful to compensate them with illusory honors. He had, in short, to play a part, straight-faced, in the tricky game that he had conceived. Saint-Simon never quite understood this. He saw clearly enough that the king was intent on debasing the peerage, but he could not imagine why a sovereign so disposed should ever defend the rights of his nobles. For example, when Madame de Torcy, the wife of a cabinet minister, took the seat of the Duchesse de Duras at the royal supper, the king, to Saint-Simon's astonishment, was irate, and delivered a public lecture on the high rank of dukes, describing it as first in the state and assuring his listeners that he could find no higher honor to bestow on his own family. Anyone, he concluded grandly, refusing honors to a duke was refusing them to *him*. "Those were his very words!" exclaims the gratified Saint-Simon. But it is perfectly evident to us that if the Torcys were to be given the actual political power while the Durases had to be content with seats at the supper table, the full weight of royal authority was needed to sustain the illusion that these seats had any value. The royal game worked, and as we shall see, Saint-Simon himself became a typical victim.

The first recorded conversation between the memoirist and the king occurred in 1693. The young officer had to thank his commander-in-chief for the appointment of a cavalry regiment, and Majesty responded "most obligingly." Saint-Simon was then eighteen and his sovereign fifty-four. He was to remain within the latter's daily sight at court, with infrequent intermissions, for the ensuing twenty-two years. Yet in all that time he was granted only three private audiences. The balance of the relationship between king and courtier was made up of nods, bows, smiles, occasional gracious words and occasional (terrible to relate) long, icy stares. Louis XIV, like a god, was sparing of his personal contacts.

On the death of his father in the same year, Saint-Simon obtained royal assent to the renewal of the family offices. At the *coucher* he approached the bed and related (probably in too great detail) the story of the paternal last moments. The king, who knew how to "season his graces," admonished the new duke to be sensible and to behave properly and promised in return that he would look out for him. It was a good enough start, but Saint-Simon pushed his luck. His first request was for a transfer to another regiment so that he would not have to serve under the Duc de Luxembourg with whom he was already engaged in a lawsuit. He not only wrote to the king about it; he followed him to mass and thence to his carriage. Louis XIV observed the hovering figure, and turned back to assure him: "I have your letter, and I shall remember." Immediately afterwards Saint-Simon received his transfer, but I wonder if he had not already etched his portrait on the royal memory as a litigious young man who took himself and his dignity a good deal too seriously.

If he had not, he surely did at their next recorded talk. By then he was married to a daughter of the Maréchal de Lorges, a discreet, virtuous, strong-minded young woman who in her quiet way watched over her husband's rank as carefully as he did himself. There was always trouble with the House of Lorraine (the Guises) who claimed the status of foreign princes, although really only peers of France, and Madame de Saint-Simon reported to her husband that a slight misunderstanding about places at table had been blown up to the king as a deliberate usurpation on her part. Saint-Simon, boiling over, approached the king at the *coucher* after he had undressed and was standing by the fireplace to bid good night to those excluded from the *petit coucher*. Louis XIV leaned gravely down to give ear to his excited subject, staring quietly while the latter expostulated on the whole misunderstanding "without omitting a single circumstance." At the end he was graciously moved to reply: "That's quite all right, sir. I realize there's nothing in it." Saint-Simon retired before the royal nod and smile, but, suddenly exploding again, he hurried back to assure the king that every word he had told him was the absolute truth. Majesty accorded him another polite dismissal. Always the wise headmaster, Louis XIV never minimized or pooh-poohed the quarrels among his boys. But he had his own opinion of them.

Saint-Simon, unhappily for himself, was soon to prove more than simply importunate. He became downright irritating. Discouraged by lack of promotion, he resigned his commission. Louis XIV liked to keep his young nobles in the army; it was the only way that he could get any use out of them. "Here is another deserter!" he exclaimed peevishly when he read the duke's letter. That night at the *coucher*, he named Saint-Simon to hold the candlestick, as if nothing had happened, but it was the last time that he did so. For the next three years he not only excluded Saint-Simon from the coveted weekends at Marly; he refused to speak to him in public or even so much as look at him. It is interesting to note that Madame de Saint-Simon continued to be included in the royal suppers. She was evidently a young woman who knew how to play her cards.

Still worse, however, was to come. The episode of the alms bag finally brought down on Saint-Simon's unsuspecting head the first overt expression of the terrible royal wrath. Once again it was the Lorraines who started it. On certain days when the king went to mass it was the custom for a lady of the court, named by the Duchesse de Bourgogne, to hand around the alms bag. Princesses of the blood were exempt from the duty, and the ladies of Lorraine, always on the lookout for an opportunity to identify themselves with royalty, began to evade it on various specious excuses. The duchesses, alerted by the watchful Saint-Simon, promptly began to evade it also, and when word of this came to the king, he really blew up. He was heard to exclaim that ever since Saint-Simon had quit his service he had done nothing but "study questions of rank and precedence and dispute with people about them," that he was the origin of all this trouble and that it might be a good idea to send him away where he could cause no more. When this terrifying threat was reported to Saint-Simon, he knew that he was in the direst straits. He consulted the chancellor and was advised to seek the extreme remedy of a private audience (his former talks with the king had been in public). "It was no light thing," he relates, "for a young man so thoroughly out of favor to go up to the king and ask abruptly for an interview," but he plucked up his courage and went to await the king's passage to his private room after dinner. He then asked permission to follow him, and the king, without a word, led him to a window embrasure where he listened in angry silence while Saint-Simon rattled on about the outrageous presumptions of the Lorraines and his own exemplary conduct. Louis XIV cared very little for anyone's precedence but his own. At last he cut through the expostulations to the central point of discipline:

> "But," interrupted the king, in the same haughty and angry manner, "you have been making speeches." "No, Sir," I said, "I have made none." "What, you have not been talking?" and he was going on in a loud voice, when I ventured to interrupt him in my turn, and, raising my voice above his: "No, Sir," I said, "I have made no speeches; if I had I would confess it to your Majesty, just as I have confessed what caused my wife to avoid making the collection, and prevented other Duchesses from doing so. But I beg you most earnestly, Sire, to believe that if I had thought for a moment that it was your Majesty's wish, I would have made the collection myself in a dish, like a village sexton."

That was the note to strike! Louis XIV was immediately mollified:

> The king then assumed an air of kindness and familiarity, and told me several times, in a thoroughly gracious tone, that that was the right way to think and speak, with other polite speeches of the sort.

Saint-Simon explains that such accounts are the best way to learn about a monarch "so difficult to approach and so terrifying even to his intimates." The audience appears to have salvaged his position at court, and the following year, when he had an operation on his arm, the king "overwhelmed me with kindnesses." In 1706, when there was a question of an embassy to Rome, it was even reported to Saint-Simon that the king was going to appoint him, having observed that he was "young but capable," but nothing came of it.

Only two years later, however, we find him in trouble again. It was reported to the king that he had made a bet that the town of Lille, then invested by the allies under Marlborough, would fall before the French could raise the siege, and he suffered a second period of disgrace. Imagining himself, as usual, the victim of numerous cabals, he again sought a private audience, but this time the king, knowing what he was in for, tried to ward it off. "What does he want to tell me?" he protested impatiently to the Maréchal de Villars. "It's all nothing. Oh, true, I've had a couple of minor complaints about him, but nothing to amount to anything. Tell him to *relax!*" But Saint-Simon was determined on his audience, and of course, he got it. Was it not the right of every schoolboy? He found the king alone, sitting at his counsel table "as was his habit when he wished to converse with someone at his ease and leisure." Whatever else he may have anticipated from the interview, Louis XIV knew that it was not going to be brief.

Saint-Simon began very foolishly. He complained about his exclusion from the Marly weekends. It was an impertinence, of course, for a courtier to assume that the sovereign even noticed him enough to exclude him. The king retorted stiffly that such things meant nothing at all. Saint-Simon then begged permission to "unburden his heart" about all the ways in which he had been misrepresented to the king. But Louis XIV cared nothing for all that. He reverted to his role of headmaster:

> Here the king interrupted: "But you know, sir, you are given to talking and finding fault; that is why people say things against you." I replied that I tried hard to avoid speaking evil of any one; as for speaking evil of His Majesty, I would die first (looking at him ardently as I spoke, straight in the face); as to other people, I said that, though I was very careful, it was very hard at times not to speak my mind naturally. "But," said the king, "you talk about everything, especially about public affairs when they are not prosperous, with bitterness and —." Here, observing that he spoke more kindly, I interrupted him in my turn. I told him that I spoke very little about public affairs, and then very cautiously; but it was true that sometimes, irritated by our misfortunes, I had expressed myself rather strongly.

Saint-Simon then proceeded to tell the poor king in detail the whole background (including the military situation) of his bet about Lille. He went on from here to a good many other matters, describing complaints, actual or imagined, against himself, and giving exhaustive explanations and defenses. He even seized the occasion to review the old episode of the alms bag and to get in some more gibes at the House of Lorraine. The king was reduced to what one imagines to have been a stupefied silence. But it was far better to bore the king than to anger him. Louis XIV did not really mind being bored. What he wanted was submission, and when he had that, he could be very gracious:

> "That only shows," said the king, in a really fatherly manner, "what sort of a reputation you have in the world, and you must admit that, to a certain extent, you deserve it. If you had never been mixed up in any of these affairs, or, at any rate, if you had not taken sides so warmly and shown yourself so touchy about questions of precedence, people would not say such things. That shows you also how careful you must be in your conduct, so as to let this impression of you fade away, and not give people any pretext for talking about you."

The little duke almost broke down before this sudden beneficence of his liege lord. It is all very well for us to smile today, but we were not brought up in a society where the monarch and the nation were synonymous.

Saint-Simon was highly critical of Louis XIV, but, like so many of his contemporaries, he had a deep need to reverence him:

> I then went on to speak of my long absence, caused by my grief at thinking that I had incurred his displeasure; and I took the opportunity to go beyond the ordinary terms of respect to express my affectionate attachment to his person, which I did with a sort of frank familiarity; for I perceived, from his looks and manner, and the way in which he spoke, that I might safely venture on it. My remarks were received with a cordiality which astonished me, and I felt satisfied that I had regained his good opinion. Seeing that I had no more to say, he rose from the table; I begged him to remember me if there were any vacant quarters in the *château*, so that I might be able to pay my court to him more assiduously. He replied that there were none vacant at present; and, bowing slightly, with a smiling and gracious air, he went into his further rooms.

This is the climax of Saint-Simon's loyalty to the crown. The critical peer, so conscious of ducal rights and prerogatives, was now humbly begging for a suite of those tiny, ill-ventilated rooms for which the greatest names in the land happily deserted their ancestral acres. But his loyalty was soon to be put to a heavy test, for the old king was engaged in the touchy business of promoting his bastards to royal rank.

Succession to the French crown was governed by the Salic law; only males descended in the male line from a king were qualified to reign. The sons and grandsons of a king were known as sons and grandsons of France, more remote descendants as princes of the blood. Royal bastards had no status whatever unless made peers by the king; normally, they could never hope to be princes. Louis XIV had four such bastards by Madame de Montespan, two sons and two daughters, who were constantly begging him for advancement, aided and abetted by their father's morganatic wife, Madame de Maintenon, formerly their governess. It had proved impossible to ally the daughters suitably abroad (William of Orange had incurred the lasting resentment of the king by refusing the offer of one of them with a crude retort), but they had been duly married off to subservient princes of the blood at home. By thus forcing his daughters into the royal family, the king hoped to ease the way for the ultimate inclusion of their brothers, the Duc du Maine and the Comte de Toulouse. In the meantime the latter occupied a sort of limbo between the peers and the princes. To Saint-Simon, who watched their gradual encroachment with passionate jealousy, it represented a threat to the very existence of orderly society. For once, he had the court with him. To place a bastard in line to the throne, even at the bottom of a considerable list of legitimate heirs, was deeply shocking to everybody. As Saint-Simon points out, if the sovereign could add a bastard to the royal family, could he not place him *ahead* of the royal family? What was to stop him, then, from naming his own successor? And in that event what happened to the principle of lineal succession on which both feudal *and* monarchical society were based? Louis XIV had finally gone too far.

But he knew it. He was old and weary of the importunities of Madame de Maintenon and Maine. He warned them that these new honors would not survive his death. He recognized that his entire court was bound to be with Saint-Simon. After all, like himself, they owed everything to birth. To have resented their attitude would have been idle. All he could do was to placate them by promoting his sons as gradually as possible in the time that remained to him and by obtaining the grudging approval of his court for each step. The sanction of so famous a stickler for precedent as Saint-Simon would be of especial help. The great monarch at last had need of the little duke, and the royal system was again invoked to bring him into line. Saint-Simon found these days that he was always included on the weekends at Marly.

Of course, he had to pay for it. When the king ordained that the children of the Duc du Maine should enjoy the same rank and honors as their father and let it be known that he wished the court to congratulate his son, Saint-Simon was on the spot. As he says: "I had only lately made my peace with the king, and he had warned me to be very careful in all matters affecting my dignity." The entire court was congratulating Maine; to have held off would have meant ruin. He resolved at last to "drain the cup to the dregs," and called upon Monsieur du Maine when the crowd in the latter's apartments was at its maximum, made his hurried bow and slipped away without a word. But nothing at Versailles escaped the royal eye. His visit was immediately reported to the king who was much pleased and remarked that "since *that* man approved of what had been done, there could be no great objection to it." Poor Saint-Simon had been used to make orthodox what he deemed the greatest heresy. It was what happened to dukes at Versailles.

Worse was to come. The Duc de Berri, son of "Monseigneur," the dauphin, had married a daughter of the Duc d'Orléans, and the question arose of the appointment of her lady of honor. Madame de Saint-Simon was rumored to be the king's choice because she was a person of irreproachable virtue (rare at court) and because she was not associated with any cabal. Saint-Simon, when sounded out by the Duc d'Orléans, placed his objections tactfully on the ground that it was a position of the second place (the Duchesse de Berri was ranked by the Duchesse de Bourgogne), but it is fairly evident that his real objection was that the Duchesse de Berri's mother, the Duchesse d'Orléans, was a royal bastard. The royal will, however, could be blunt. "Would you refuse it?" the Duc d'Orléans demanded. Saint-Simon had to admit that, as a loyal subject, he would, of course, obey the express commands of his sovereign. The next he heard of the matter was the appointment itself.

> On his way back the king called to me in the Gallery, and told me to follow him into his room, as he wished to speak to me. He advanced to a little table against the wall, at some distance from the other persons present, on the side nearest the Gallery from which he had entered. There he told me that he had selected Madame de Saint-Simon to be Lady of Honor to the future Duchesse de Berri; that it was a special mark of his esteem for her virtue and merit to entrust to her charge, at the age of thirty-two, a Princess of such tender age and so nearly related to himself; moreover, by bringing me into closer access to himself he intended to show me that he was quite convinced of the sincerity with which I had spoken to him a few months ago.

Saint-Simon made a "moderately low bow" and replied "laconically" that he felt deeply the honor so placed in his wife and himself. He assumed that the king would understand immediately from his manner that he was accepting a degrading job from motives of pure loyalty. But the Saint-Simons of this world can never believe that others do not share their petty standards. I doubt if Louis XIV had any reaction to the "laconic" quality of the verbose little duke's reply other than a faint surprise and relief. Certainly there was no apology in his next remark: "But you must keep your tongue in order." Saint-Simon, however, replied "boldly" that he *had* kept it in order and would continue to do so in the future. By this he meant the king to infer that he had not been publicly complaining about the humiliation of his wife's expected appointment! Louis XIV simply smiled, "with a more satisfied expression," and turned to announce the appointment to the rest of the company.

But the nadir was reached in the final year of the old king's reign when the bastards were at last officially raised to the rank of princes of the blood with rights of succession to the crown. Death had played havoc with the king's direct heirs; only a delicate great-grandson, a nephew and one great-nephew stood between the princes of the house of Condé and the throne. As the latter were but remotely related to Louis XIV, having to trace their line all the way back to Saint Louis to find a royal progenitor, a conflict could be foreseen between them and the bastards, who were at least the natural children of a sovereign. Here was despotism, in Saint-Simon's eyes, worse than Peter the Great's. But what did he do about it? Just what Peter the Great's subjects would have done. Accompanying the whole court, whose cringing servility he did not scruple to excoriate, he went to the apartments of the Duc du Maine to congratulate him "*very sincerely*"!

The phrase, however, is not sarcastic; he explains that what he had really resented about the bastards was their intermediate rank between the royal family and the peerage. If they were merged with royalty, the peerage moved back up to its traditional second place. But he does not for a moment convince us that this was the real reason that he bowed to Maine. The real reason was that the king had "fixed his eyes steadily on him" during the supper that had preceded the congratulatory visit. Victory was again with the monarch, but it was his last.

The wise but misguided old sovereign was correct in his warning to his bastard sons that their new-found honors would not survive his death. By will he attempted to give Maine supervision of the young king during his minority and a focal seat on the council that was intended to act as a brake to the regent's power. All this was swept away by the Duc d'Orléans as soon as his royal uncle was dead, without so much as a murmur of opposition. And worse retribution was to come. Only three years after the end of the reign, at a Bed of Justice, the bastards were stripped of their princely ranks and privileges and reduced to the grade in the nobility to which their recently created peerages entitled them. Saint-Simon, who, as a friend of the regent's, had been instrumental in bringing this about, viewed the proceedings of the Bed of Justice in a passage of his memoirs that reads like a shrill *Nunc Dimittis:*

> I truly felt as though I were going to swoon, for my heart seemed to swell within me and could find no room in which to expand. I remembered the long days and years of servitude, those unhappy times when, like a victim, I was dragged to the Parlement to witness the triumph of the bastards, as they rose by degrees to a pinnacle above our heads. Then I thought of this day of law and justice, this dreadful retribution which had elevated us by the force of recoil. I could rightly congratulate myself that all this had been brought about by me. I triumphed, I was avenged, I rejoiced in my vengeance. I delighted in the satisfaction of my strongest, most eager and most steadfast desires!

But even if the bastards had retained their royal rank, as matters turned out, they would never have succeeded to the crown. The direct royal line and the Houses of Orléans and Condé continued to produce heirs while the illegitimate branches withered. Maine had two sons but no grandchildren, while Toulouse had one son whose heiress became Duchesse d'Orléans. Thus the great fortune of the bastards, which had originated in the will which Louis XIV had obliged his unhappy cousin, the Grande Mademoiselle, to make in favor of the Duc du

Maine as the price of her lover's liberty, reverted by natural succession to the royal line from which it had been raped. The flaw in the great king's monarchical system was catharized by time. Only revolution could now destroy it. From the death of Mazarin, when Louis XIV took over the reins of government, to the fall of the Bastille, it lasted one hundred and twenty-eight years. For all its mammoth faults it held France together as no other system of government has done, before or since.

Because he foresaw the pernicious effects of a bureaucratic government centered about an absolute monarch, Saint-Simon is often given more credit for political vaticination than he strictly deserves. We should remember that his own political solution was simply to restore the power of the nobles. It was the purest feudalism, and almost nobody but Saint-Simon, including his fellow peers, really wanted it. He was like a shrill Wall Street Republican in the days of the New Deal, predicting, with some accuracy, the evil consequences of red tape and high taxes, but recommending in their stead a return to the old, discredited system of laisser faire. The government of Louis XIV was at least an effort to cope with contemporary problems, while Saint-Simon, for all his perspicacity, had his eyes fixed on the past. One wonders if his project of restoring the feudal hierarchy would not have summoned a Robespierre from the masses a century before his time.

Meredith Reassailed

George Meredith is to me the most constantly disappointing novelist of the last century, for I can never quite bring myself to abandon the hope that somewhere along the sizable shelf of his fiction I may find another *Egoist* or at least another *Diana*. How is it conceivable that the author of two such perfect novels should never, in a long and productive life, have repeated his double success? And so, every few years, I find myself giving him another chance in the presumptuous tribunal of my literary taste. Perhaps in the past I was too young or too hasty. Perhaps it takes maturity to savor a vintage Meredith. I remind myself how many critics used to scoff at the later style of Henry James and how sacrosanct it has since become. Little by little I wax enthusiastic at the prospect of enrolling myself among a gentle elite who will rediscover the subtle beauties of *One of Our Conquerors* and gather to worship at the shrine of a new "old master." Along the stock exchange of literature I seem to hear the cry ring out: "Buy Meredith!"

But my experience is always the same. I make a good enough start with *The Ordeal of Richard Feverel*, though I find I like it less at each reading, tiring of the iteration of the evil effects of Sir Austin's manifestly absurd system of education. And I am mildly diverted by the trials of the snobbish sisters in *Evan Harrington*, though again I sense the cannon in combat with the mosquito. They are early works and well enough, but I am soon ready to push on. Yet it is at just this point, when I feel that my real pleasure must be about to begin, that all pleasure abruptly ceases. I have traversed the field in my search of water, but I hit a rocky beach in a curious little novel, *Rhoda Fleming*, where a handsome farmer foils the villain by the old stratagem of suddenly producing the villain's first wife. It has hardly any of Meredith's characteristics; one is put in mind of Trollope trying to ape Hardy. Then come the confused, episodic Emilia stories, *Sandra Belloni* and *Vittoria*, and a long picaresque novel, *Harry Richmond*, which, located in the history of fiction midway between *Tom Jones* and *Augie March*, causes one to speculate if broadness in matters of sex is not a quality indispensable to that type of tale. Is not a Victorian picaresque novel, to put it more bluntly, something of a contradiction in terms? I next stub my toe on *Beauchamp's Career*, the dullest and most difficult yet, but at least it brings me to the water's edge of the later style, and my hope revives. I just manage to float with *The Tragic Comedians* and *Lord Ormont and his Aminta*, each founded on a historical incident, though I cannot but wonder what failure of imagination was responsible for Meredith's new method of selecting *données*, which seems the equivalent of picking them from a book of opera synopses. *The Amazing Marriage* is choppier water, and *One of Our Conquerors* a towering breaker which, no matter how artfully I dive into it, will always pick me up and fling me back, panting and exhausted, on the sands of my determination. Not even that strongest of all drives, the ambition (a relict of school days) to be able to tell the world that I have read *all* of Meredith, can give me strength enough to get through it.

Well, the reader may say, so you don't like Meredith. Is that so worthy of note? Hasn't he, notoriously, always had his detractors and his admirers? Siegfried Sassoon says that "when people dislike Meredith it is useless to argue with them." J. B. Priestley goes further; he suggests that they have dubbed themselves incompetent readers, adding that one can spot them by their preference for *Rhoda Fleming*. But I *do* like Meredith, and I *don't* like *Rhoda Fleming!* I would happily rank *The Egoist* among the ten finest novels in the English tongue. Is that not enough to take me out of Mr Priestley's cage of Philistines? And turning briskly the pages of his and Sassoon's books on the subject, I note with interest, even with a wry satisfaction, that they appear to have the same trouble reading Meredith that I do. Sassoon admits freely that Meredith groaned under the tyranny of the three-volume novel, that much of what he wrote was "rubble and fustian" and that whole chapters of *Harry Richmond* are "labored and without momentum." Both agree that the style of the later novels is absurdly convoluted and pointlessly, perhaps intentionally, obscure. Priestley is the harsher of the two. To him *One of Our Conquerors* is "a charnel house of slain English" and its author, quite simply, "one of the worst narrators in the history of the English novel." He concludes:

> . . . his manner and style, especially in the later novels, refuse to undertake what might be called the donkey-work of narration. He will go miles out of his way, giving us pages of what can only be considered sheer bad writing, in order to avoid making a few plain statements of fact, necessary for the conduct of the narrative.

For all this plain talking, however, both critics remain stubborn admirers of Meredith's fiction. Why? Priestley praises the curious dichotomy that Meredith creates by placing romantic figures against an intellectual background, a procedure which compels the reader to follow the comic spirit with a philosophic eye and which imbues even the scenes of greatest sentiment with the bitter-sweet flavor of irony. I have no quarrel with this; I find it, on the contrary, well put. But where I differ fundamentally with Messrs. Sassoon and Priestley is in the low value which they ascribe to narrative. To say that a storyteller cannot tell a story is to me like saying that a painter cannot paint. I am too much of a Jacobite to have any patience with a novel that does not hold together as a novel. James may have paid a handsome posthumous tribute to Meredith ("He did the best things best") but hear his opinion of *Lord Ormont and his Aminta:*

> The unspeakable Lord Ormont has roused me to critical rage. Not a difficulty met, not a figure presented, not a scene constituted — not a dim shadow condensing once into audible or visible reality — making you hear for an instant the tap of its feet on the earth.

I might plead an exception for Lord Ormont's sister, Lady Charlotte; surely I hear the tap of *her* feet in the wonderful scenes where she tries to bully her grandson's tutor. But, like James, I cannot read a novel for the sake of a few good scenes. The prospect of Lady Charlotte will not compensate me for her creator's failure to interest me in his basic theme: why an old man should refuse to acknowledge his beautiful young wife before the world. By the time I come to the answer, I have lost interest largely because Meredith seems to have lost his. And by like token I cannot feel rewarded by the beautiful descriptions of Alpine scenery in *The Amazing Marriage* when I don't care about the marriage itself. It seems to me that scenery must be secondary, unless it constitutes an integral part of the action. And, worse still, once dullness has set in, I can no longer properly respond to a passage of good writing, which, extracted from the context, might well delight me. It's as if, in a boring play, one of the characters should suddenly recite the "Ode to a Nightingale."

Yet so low does Priestley hold the virtue of storytelling that he does not hesitate to judge *all* of Meredith's work as wanting in it. "Regarded as a narrative," he states flatly, "every novel that Meredith wrote is not merely faulty but downright bad, even perverse in its badness." Now this, I submit, is simply not the case. In fact, my whole thesis is just that *Diana of the Crossways* and *The Egoist* are superlative narratives, elaborately conceived and carefully organized, and for that very reason constitute the only frames in which I can still admire the genius of Meredith with any continuing pleasure. And I would argue further that the reason the other novels, with the exception of *Richard Feverel*, have lost their modern audience is that they are poor narratives or barely narratives at all.

Diana, it is true, has often been criticized as a story. Why does Diana marry Warwick, in the first place? And why does she ruin her second chance for happiness by selling to the press a cabinet secret, told her in confidence by the man she loves? But these are not truly questions of narrative, but rather of the author's success in delineating his central character. The problem of the sale of the cabinet secret is the whole *donnée* of the novel. The task which Meredith set for himself was to create a woman of wit, intellect, noble character and integrity who would nevertheless be guilty of such an act. Now it may be that he has not wholly succeeded, for his task, in my opinion, was insuperable, but, unlike the tasks which he set for himself in the later novels, it at least fascinated him. Consequently, Diana fascinates us, and if her creator does not quite convince us of her midnight trip to the editor's office, his failure does not affect our pleasure in the balance of her tale. Everything in the novel is directed toward giving us a heightened sense of her beauty and charm; the very speed of the prose is designed to make us feel the quickness of her wit (much more than the examples of it) and the suddenness of her impulses. The beauty of the English countryside becomes Diana's beauty, as does the beauty of Lord Melbourne's London. Much time is covered and much space traversed, but there is a fine unity of mood utterly lacking in the earlier books. James's statement that Meredith harnessed "winged horses to the heavy car of fiction" applies particularly, perhaps uniquely, to *Diana*.

If *Diana*, then, is a novel of rapid movement and changing scene, *The Egoist* is one of gravely measured tempo and concentrated action. If the heroine of the first is a swallow that needs to soar, the hero of the other is a rooster that can only strut. Meredith fixes our eye firmly upon the latter at the outset by showing us Sir Willoughby in the center of his demesne, in his great hall surrounded by dependent relatives and servitors, the benign and beaming young baronet, the adored of the countryside, the matrimonial catch of catches, who has everything ready for a triumphant journey through life — except a wife to share the ride. Imagine the fluttering hearts of Jane Austen's mothers! All of the major characters, including the heroine, are either Sir Willoughby's house guests or residents on his estate. The terrifying Mrs. Mountstuart Jenkinson alone occupies a position of independence; she is a neighbor, for she must represent the forces of the great outside world which Sir Willoughby, petty despot and bully that he is at heart, knows that he must placate. Meredith has not had to conceive a duke in a castle or even a duchess to quell his hero; all he needs is a neighboring dowager with a sharp eye and a sharp tongue, brisk, rude and very conservative, but on the side of the angels (at least of an angel like Clara) if the angels have only the courage to state their case. She is not infallible; she can be fooled, but Sir Willoughby must work to fool her. She is no maiden aunt. A "rogue in porcelain" is her verdict of Clara, and the phrase is Sir Willoughby's doom, as he dimly but frantically suspects from the very beginning.

Meredith thus announces his theme: why should such a paragon, such a cynosure, have such difficulty finding a mate? Why should he be jilted, once, twice, *thrice?* The closely knit working out of the answer against the bright backdrop of a green park and a soft old mansion by characters who enunciate with a high clarity of tone gives to the novel some of the pleasing artificiality of a perfectly produced English comedy of manners. Indeed, from the entrance of Clara to the final curtain the dramatic unities are carefully observed. Oh, true, the action occupies several weeks rather than a day, and the characters go off the estate to dine at Mrs. Mountstuart's and poor Clara gets as far as the railway station in her desperate effort to escape her fate, but essentially we are watching one group of persons against one setting at one point of time. And the advantage of adhering to the unities is that once the stage has been set and the central idea exposed, Meredith can let his ideas spill over the setting in any shape he chooses. He can buttonhole us like Thackeray and lecture us on comedy and wines; he can take wing into the romantic or he can roll about in what approaches farce — everything seems only to enrich his theme and to heighten our enjoyment of it. And as we progress through the tale the atmosphere seems less and less artificial in the growingly intensified glare of the light which is remorselessly held on the unfortunate Willoughby. It has been said that in actual life he would have had no difficulty finding a suitable mate. Perhaps it is Meredith's triumph that makes one doubt this, but hasn't one seen just such men, men who appear to be fatally driven to the very women who will not have them? For it is not simply that Willoughby is an egoist, a pompous ass. He cannot love — one is almost tempted to see his drama as a tragedy of impotence. As the unhappy man writhes and turns in his frantic search for the increasingly elusive spouse, as he is driven at last to face a bleak and loveless marriage in order to have a bride, *any* bride, whose hand he can hold up to the approaching Mrs. Mountstuart, the world incarnate, glimpsed through a window descending from her carriage as he kneels to the obdurate Laetitia, we begin to shudder in our laughter. The picture of the poor, deflated rooster, his comb drooping, groveling before the drabbest hen in the barnyard, can no longer be viewed with complete detachment. As Priestley says, Sir Willoughby has taken on some of the quality of Everyman.

No sooner have I come to this point and put down my pen to reflect on the beauties of *The Egoist* than I feel once more the prick of my old, periodic urge to revisit Meredith. I scan those thirteen novels on the shelf, of which eleven continue to elude me. How could there not be pleasures still in store? Maybe I was prejudiced because I wanted to be clever and write this article. Maybe if I try again, without the vanity of prospective authorship, maybe if I am patient and relaxed, maybe if I am humble, the secret garden will be unlocked. And I find my hand stealing up again toward *Sandra Belloni*. Perhaps this time I will succeed.

Proust's Picture of Society

Gore Vidal once told me that in reading Proust he was put off by a nagging sense that the narrator was a conjurer with three balls in the air, busily engaged in the triple misrepresentation that he was not a homosexual, not a social climber and not a Jew. Of course, one can answer that Proust, as a novelist, was under no obligation to endow any character, even the "I" who tells his story, with his own characteristics, but he deliberately invites the identification by giving the narrator his own first name. And when we consider George Painter's exhaustive researches (*Proust: The Early Years*) to prove that every character, every episode, even every landscape, has a corresponding model or models drawn from the author's own experience, when we consider further how little point there would be in writing so many volumes to recapture a purely invented past, we must conclude that the whole work, if not, strictly speaking, an autobiography, is at least bathed in a more intimately subjective light than other novels. It seems to me a consequence that to read the book against the background of the author's known predilections and prejudices becomes something more than the usual academic game of scholarship. It becomes a process that brings the picture into clearer focus.

To take up the first of the misrepresentations, it is now, of course, so notorious that Proust was homosexual that the number of his readers who are ignorant of the fact must be relatively small. Certainly, anyone trying to read the story of Marcel as that of a sexually normal male will be faced with some baffling questions. Why, for example, does Marcel fall in love with Albertine only when Doctor Cottard points out to him that, while dancing with another girl, she is rubbing her breasts against those of her partner? And why does Marcel's mother, who is otherwise represented as a woman of the strictest Victorian morality, tolerate the presence of Albertine in her apartment at night? Why is almost every male character in the book, other than the narrator, an actual or reputed homosexual? A perspicacious reader who knew nothing of Proust's personal life would probably recognize in the author (as the author recognizes in Charlus) the tendency of the homosexual to attribute his tastes to others. But what of the other two misrepresentations? Would the same perspicacious reader become aware that the author was half Jewish and a man who had spent much of his life assiduously cultivating a titled, anti-Semitic aristocracy? It seems less likely.

What difference does it make? Not much, surely, in an appreciation of the work as a whole. But it seems to me that there are certain exaggerations in Proust's picture of the social world that stem directly from his confusion of his snobbishness with his love of history and art, and that an analysis of these exaggerations may be of assistance to the reader, who, like myself, has speculated about them.

I note at the outset that the characters of *À la Recherche du Temps Perdu* are constantly referring to Saint-Simon. Marcel's grandfather is as familiar with everything concerning the bourgeoisie of Combray as was Saint-Simon's Prince de Conti with the family tree of the court. Swann, in the torments of his jealousy, emigrates to "those few and distant parts of himself which had remained almost foreign to his love and to his pain," by reading about court life in Saint-Simon. In his first appearance in the novel he refers to Saint-Simon's volume on the mission to Spain. The relationship of Léonie and her maid, Françoise, is described as a counterpart to the relationship between king and courtiers at Versailles, and the perfect manners, the ceremoniousness, the ignorance and the heartlessness of the Duc de Guermantes is contrasted with Saint-Simon's portrait of Louis XIV.

Indeed, the Duke occupies in the novel the same position at the apex of society that the sun king does in the memoirs. Even Albertine loves talking to Marcel about Saint-Simon. But the character, of course, who revels most in the many volumes of the prolific duke is the Baron de Charlus. He is the successor of those great gentlemen in the memoirs who associate with their lackeys because no one else is good enough for them. As an expert in his own genealogy and as a zealous watcher of any usurped privilege, he excels Saint-Simon himself, for he claims precedence for the Guermantes over the House of France. He brings the past into constant, immediate relation with himself ("There are portraits of my uncles, the King of Poland and the King of England, by Mignard") and amuses himself at parties by creating a sort of tableau-vivant out of the memoirs. We see him at Madame Verdurin's, refusing to rise from his chair when his hostess comes over to speak to him, impersonating in his fancy the Maréchal d'Uxelles who was so proud as to remain seated, under a pretense of laziness, before the most distinguished persons at court. It is a game which I suspect that the author himself may have enjoyed playing at Robert de Montesquiou's or at the Comtesse Greffuhle's. And when, at the end of *Le Temps Retrouvé,* Marcel describes the great literary work which he hopes he may be spared long enough to undertake, which is, of course, no other than the one which the reader is then completing, he feels it necessary to state that he has no intention of reproducing the memoirs of Saint-Simon.

Nor is it my intent to imply that he was. That he might have done so, had he chosen, is demonstrated by the brilliant parody of Saint-Simon in *Pastiches et Mélanges,* where he mixes characters from the court of Versailles with his own acquaintances. I do maintain, however, that he dignified and excused his own snobbishness by identifying it with the snobbishness of Saint-Simon and by consciously adopting the role of court historian to a latter-day Versailles. It was a habit of mind and attitude that distorted his over-all picture of society in three respects.

In the first place, his society characters have a hardness, a rudeness and a maliciousness that is more in keeping with a crowded, jealous court than with life in a large modern city. When Madame de Gallardon speaks to her cousin Oriane about Swann, whom she knows to be the latter's dearest friend, she says: "People do say about your M. Swann that he's the sort of man one can't have in the house, is that true?" The author explains this ill-tempered outburst to a woman whose favor the speaker is anxious to cultivate by describing the latter as one of those persons who can never restrain her highest social ambitions "to the immediate and secret satisfaction of saying something disagreeable." Now this is all very well, and one has known plenty of Mesdames de Gallardon, but my trouble comes from the fact that we *body* in Proust seems to be able to resist the temptation to say something disagreeable. The air is more the arrogant air of Versailles than that of Paris within the memory of many still living. When the Baron de Charlus' friends come to Madame Verdurin's to hear Morel, their offensiveness is hard to credit. Typical of the comments, Proust tells us, of each duchess within the hearing of their hostess are: "Show me, which is mother Verdurin; do you think I really need speak to her? I do hope, at least, that she won't put my name in the paper tomorrow, nobody would ever speak to me again. What! That woman with the white hair, but she looks quite presentable," or "Tell me, has there ever been a Monsieur Verdurin?" Poor Odette, in her helpless old age, is treated even worse:

> One constantly heard people say: "I don't know if Madame de Forcheville recognizes me, perhaps I ought to be introduced over again." "You can dispense with that" (someone replied at the top of his voice, neither knowing nor caring that Gilberte's mother could hear every word), "you won't get any fun out of it. She's a bit daft."

The characters behave with a heartlessness about illness and death that recalls Saint-Simon's passages on the deaths of Louis XIV's heirs. The Duc de Guermantes refuses to be told of the death of a cousin because he would have to give up a ball; his wife at the same time affects not to credit Swann's news of his own impending demise, and Madame Verdurin, confronted inescapably with the death of her friend, Princess Sherbatoff, pretends always to have disliked her rather than put on a mourning air that might dampen her party. The Verdurins, indeed, have no mercy even on physical disabilities, as is shown by their treatment of Saniette:

> "What's that he says?" shouted Monsieur Verdurin with an air of disgust and fury combined, knitting his brows as though it was all he could do to grasp something unintelligible. "It is impossible to understand what you say, what have you got in your mouth?" he inquired, growing more and more furious, and alluding to Saniette's defective speech. "Poor Saniette, I won't have him made unhappy," said Madame Verdurin in a tone of false pity, so as to leave no one in doubt as to her husband's insolent attention.

It may be argued that Madame Verdurin is not in society at the time, but later she becomes Princesse de Guermantes. One doubts if she had to improve her manners to suit her new position. For hear Monsieur de Charlus, speaking at the Prince de Guermantes' of Madame de Saint-Euverte, whom he knows to be listening:

> "What would prevent me from questioning her about those passionate times in the acuteness of my olfactory organ. I say to myself all at once:

> Oh, good Lord, someone has broken the lid of my cesspool, which is simply the marquise opening her mouth to emit some invitation. They tell me the indefatigable old street walker gives 'garden parties.' I should describe them as invitations to explore the sewers. Are you going to wallow there?"

Conceding that Charlus is a bit insane, would not his interlocutor try to silence him, especially as she knows that poor Madame de Saint-Euverte is overhearing all? And would Madame de Saint-Euverte really fawn on the Baron after the humiliation of hearing herself described as a cesspool?

In the second place, I think it questionable if people in society in Proust's day thought and talked quite so obsessively about their social position. The members of the Guermantes family hold forth with amazing pedantry about their own genealogy. Their prototypes may have done so to Proust, but I suspect that he encouraged them. Did they to everyone? At Marcel's first dinner at the Duchesse de Guermantes' the company (though I admit to the Duchesse's disgust) turns happily from gossip to settle down for the major part of the evening to the serious business of pedigree. It is pedigree, too, at its heaviest: "Not in that way at all, she belonged to the branch of the Ducs de la Rochefoucauld, my grandmother came from the Ducs de Doudeauville," but Marcel, like his creator, is entranced and cannot even respond to the questions of the Turkish ambassadress for fear of missing any of the genealogies. To him, a great name keeps in the full light of day the men and women who bear it; one follows the course of their families, through diaries and correspondence, back to the Middle Ages to recapture a past in which "impenetrable night" would cloak the origins of middle class folk. But his aesthetic pleasure is even greater than his historical:

> The Prince d'Agrigente himself, as soon as I heard that his mother had been a Damas, a granddaughter of the Duke of Modena, was delivered, as from an unstable chemical alloy, from the face and speech that prevented one from recognizing him and went to form with Damas and Modena, which themselves were only titles, a combination infinitely more seductive. Each name displaced by the attractions of another, with which I had never suspected it of having any affinity, left the unalterable position which it had occupied in my brain, where familiarity had dulled it, and speeding to join the Mortemarts, the Stuarts or the Bourbons, traced with them branches of the most graceful design and an everchanging color.

Relating a title to the past is simply projecting snobbishness back into history. Proust was as impressed by a dead duke as by a live one. His characters have streams of consciousness that ceaselessly gurgle over the damp pebbles of rank. The young Madame de Cambremer has married her husband in order to be able to refer to her mother-in-law's brother by the family abbreviation: "Mon oncle de Ch'nouville." Madame de Villeparisis speaks with affected amusement but basic veneration of the convent where her great-aunts were abbesses, which excluded the daughters of the King of France because they were descended from the Medici. Her nephew, the Prince de Guermantes, makes a scene at every dinner party when he is not given the seat to which he would have been entitled under Louis XIV. And Charlus, of course, excels them all, speaking of his relatives who are described in Saint-Simon's memoirs as if they were contemporaries: "We took precedence over all foreign princes. The Duc de Bourgogne, having come to us with ushers with raised wands, we obtained the king's authority to have them lowered." Yet in contrast to the Courvoisiers, a related but rival clan, the Guermantes have a reputation of modernity and liberalness! The latter, whom we meet only fleetingly, are the family who are supposed to be the *real* conservatives in questions of precedence and pedigree. I am aware that there were, and still are, persons as obsessed with these questions as Charlus himself, but to postulate a whole society of them seems to approach the field of caricature.

And, finally, Proust's picture of the society of the Faubourg St.-Germain is too lush, too rich. No matter how painstakingly he underlines the dullness, the selfishness, and the fatuity of the Guermantes set, they remain to the end still invested with much of the glamour in which his imagination has clothed them. The beauty of their women, the romance of their titles and palaces, the splendor of their pedigrees give them a fairy tale quality which may be intentionally contrasted with the banality of their conversation and lives, but which nonetheless lingers in the reader's mind as an attribute somehow earned and merited by society people. It is illuminating in this respect to read a fatuous little volume by Princess Marthe Bibesco entitled *La Duchesse de Guermantes.* In Proust's portrait of Oriane she professes to recognize the blond beauty, the ancient lineage and the high style of her old friend Laure de Chevigné, and she relates an anecdote about the latter that might indeed have been taken from *Le Côté de Guermantes.* Laure de Chevigné, greeting the Grand Duchess Wladimir of Russia, treats her with a combination of old court courtesy and near impertinence that recalls the relationship between the Duchesse de Guermantes and the Princesse de Parme. Taking in the Grand Duchess' hat and dress in one sweeping glance, she exclaims: "Possible, in St. Petersburg, or the Hague, or Copenhagen. *Impossible* in Paris. I take the liberty of escorting Madame to the Rue de la Paix, to Paquin's or to Worth's. Yes, now, immediately, at this moment! Gustave! Call Her Imperial Highness' carriage!" This, admittedly, is pure Oriane, but Princess Bibesco has not a word to say about the insipidity, the selfishness or the vanity of the character with whom she is so proud to identify her old and valued friend. Yet it is not possible (however tempting to suppose) that a woman who has written three books on Proust should have failed to finish his novel. Her attitude is simply further evidence of how much of Proust's adoration of the aristocratic way of life seeps through the meshes of his analytical net.

I have been careful to set down these criticisms of Proust's picture of society because I wish to clear the way for a final judgment of undiluted praise. For never, to my knowledge, in fiction or outside of it, has there been so brilliant or so comprehensive a study of the social world. In fact, it stands so above its nearest competitors as to seem in retrospect almost the only picture of society in all of literature. Most people who write about society, whether they be novelists or sociologists or simply gossip columnists, make the basic error of assuming that there must be some consistency in its standards. They take for granted that there are rules which govern the qualifications of those seeking admission, that if one has been gently born or richly born, or if one can play polo or excel at cards, or if one has the gift of pleasing or is a good shot or a good conversationalist, one may tap with confidence at any closed gates. When the rules are seen not to apply, the observer concludes that they once did, but have since broken down. As the cases of nonapplication multiply, he is apt to shrug in frustration and say: "Oh, well, nowadays, it's only a question of money!"

What Proust alone had the patience to piece out is that any society will apply all known standards together or individually, or in any combination needed to include a maverick who happens to please or to exclude an otherwise acceptable person who happens not to. Nor are society people conscious of the least inconsistency in acting so. They keep no records, and they have no written constitution. Why should their rules be defined in any way other than by a list of exceptions to them? Proust understood this with the clarity of one who had succeeded in being accepted. There is a delightful passage in which he describes how the Baron de Charlus never hesitates to reverse himself. If a nobleman with whom he has quarreled happens to come of an ancient family possessed of a recent dukedom, the precedence of the dukedom becomes everything, the family nothing. "The Montesquious are descended from an old family?" he snorts. "What would that prove, supposing that it were proved? They have descended so far that they have reached the fourteenth storey below stairs." If, on the contrary, he has quarreled with a gentleman possessed of an ancient dukedom, but to whom this distinction has come without any length of pedigree, the case is altered, pedigree alone counts. He says of the Duc de Luynes: "I ask you; M. Alberti, who does not emerge from the mire until Louis XIII. What can it matter to us that favoritism at court allowed them to pick up dukedoms to which they have no right?" Small wonder that Madame Verdurin could not fathom the standards by which he selected her guests for Morel's recital.

Only by conceding the arbitrariness of those on top and by intuitively sensing the bonds of congeniality that hold them together can the observer hope to appreciate the different gradations in position. He must also be prepared for the bad memory of society and its habit of judging its own history by the same erroneous standards of its most misguided student. Take, in *Le Côté de Guermantes,* the contrasted positions of Madame Leroi and the Marquise de Villeparisis. Madame Leroi, the daughter of "rich timber people," has learned to copy exactly the colors of the Guermantes and the Courvoisiers and has penetrated so far into the inner citadel that only a knowledgeable minority is even aware of her existence. Madame de Villeparisis, on the other hand, though a member of the Guermantes family and once treated "like a daughter" by Queen Marie Amélie, has fallen from the first rank because of the irregularity of her life. Her parties seem smart enough to the uninitiated, because her family still attend them, as do many famous artists and men of letters, and because the talk is good. Madame de Villeparisis knows how to make her lions roar, while Madame Leroi, in the tradition of the truly fashionable, seats them at the card table. But it nevertheless remains the sad law of the social world that Madame de Villeparisis would gladly leave her lions to roar alone for the opportunity of sitting at the least of those card tables. Only after the death of both women will their fortunes be reversed. Posterity will judge Madame de Villeparisis a great social leader, because of the glittering names strewn through the pages of her memoirs, memoirs that Madame Leroi would never have stooped to write. The children of people who snubbed her will freely accord Madame de Villeparisis in history the social position that she wanted in life. They will never have heard of Madame Leroi.

The rapidly fluctuating nature of society makes it a perfect theme in a book about time. There is no stain so deep that a little time will not wash it out, no position so assured that a little time will not erode it. Marcel's favorite duchess may be "the eighteenth Oriane de Guermantes in succession, without a single mésalliance," but her reputation at the end is that of a déclasseé who hobnobs with actresses, while the niece of Jupien, the tailor, adopted by Charlus, becomes first Mlle. d'Oleron and later Marquise de Cambremer. Would anyone anticipate that Odette, a prostitute married to a friend of the Prince of Wales and the Comte de Paris, would have to await the death of her husband to be accepted by the smart set which dropped him for marrying her? Who but Proust would explain that the Baron de Charlus' reputation for homosexuality in Madame Verdurin's circle, however abundantly merited by his private life, is still undeserved because they have confused him with another Monsieur de Charlus, whose wide reputation for the same vice is unfounded? Or that Swann, who disdained to boast to Marcel's family of his brilliant position at the very summit of society, should in later years become noticeably vulgar in dropping the names of minor bureaucrats whom he has induced to call on his wife? Or that Madame Verdurin who turns all her hatred on Swann for refusing to join in her denunciation of the Duchesse de la Tremouille, whom she does not even know, should later occupy, as Princesse de Guermantes, the first position in the world she has once affected to despise? Society is not aware of changing its standards, for it has no memory except for its own acts of condemnation, and for these only so far as the individual condemned is concerned. Swann can never be forgiven for marrying Odette, but his daughter, who was not even born in wedlock, can become a Guermantes. Society is violently contrary; it hates to be wooed and fears to be despised. Marcel can be invited to the Guermantes' only when he has ceased to care about being invited. Society is kinder and less critical than he has expected, but only with its darlings; society is harder than he has expected, but only with those who fail to conceal their yearning to enter it, although it is to just this yearning that society owes what glamour and reputation it has. One of the reasons that *À la Recherche* is so long a book is that inconsistency, if described at all, must be described in detail.

Most novels that deal with society take on some of the meretricious gaudiness that it is their avowed purpose to deplore. Their authors become guilty of the snobbishness and triviality of which they accuse their characters. Octave Feuillet and Ouida may shake their heads over the empty vanity of the great world, but they revel in describing it. Proust comes closest to escaping the contamination of his subject matter because he does not set society apart from the rest of mankind. To him the differences between class and class are superficial. Snobbishness reigns on all levels, so why does it matter which level one selects to study? Why not, indeed, pick the highest level, particularly if one's own snobbishness is thus gratified? Society in Proust parades before us, having to represent not a segment of mankind, but something closer to mankind itself. It is the very boldness of Proust's assumption that his universe is *the* universe, like the boldness of his assumption that all love is jealousy and all men homosexuals, that gives to his distorted picture a certain universal validity. It is his faith that a sufficiently careful study of each part will reveal the whole, that the analysis of a dinner party can be as illuminating as the analysis of a war. It is his glory that he very nearly convinces us.

Americans in Trollope

THE GROWTH of James's opinion of Trollope, from a partiality of which he was avowedly ashamed to a rather bemused respect, is illustrated by his two descriptions of the prolific British novelist on an Atlantic voyage, one written at the time and one six years later. In a letter to his family in 1876 James relates:

> We had also Anthony Trollope, who wrote novels in his stateroom (he does it literally every morning in his life, no matter where he may be) and played cards with Mrs. Bronson all the evening. He has a gross and repulsive face and manner, but appears *bon enfant* when you talk with him. But he is the dullest Briton of them all.

His essay in 1883, after Trollope's death, in which he reassesses the departed novelist as "one of the most trustworthy, though not one of the most eloquent, of the writers who have helped the heart of man to know itself," strikes a more reverent note:

> He drove his pen as steadily on the tumbling ocean as in Montague Square. Trollope has been accused of being deficient in imagination, but in the face of such a fact as that the charge will scarcely seem just. The power to shut one's eyes, one's ears (to say nothing of another sense) upon the scenery of a pitching Cunarder and open them to the loves and sorrows of Lily Dale or the conjugal embarrassments of Lady Glencora Palliser is certainly a faculty which could take to itself wings.

So far as I know, Trollope has left no recorded version of his own impressions either of the young James or of his early work. Very likely he had none. But if he had, I should doubt if they were very favorable. Trollope would have found James too intellectual, too refined, possibly too American. For he made very little effort to conceal a stout middle class prejudice against Yankees. One is astonished today by James's own evaluation of Trollope's American characters:

> His American portraits (by the way they are several in number), are always friendly; they hit it off more happily than the attempt to depict American character from the European point of view is accustomed to do.

I can only shudder at the thought of what those less happy attempts must have been. For it seems evident to me that Trollope's American portraits, with a single exception, are the least successful of his gallery, a gallery which, taken as a whole, is to me the most glorious of Victorian fiction. It may be that the pen which could delineate with such accuracy and sympathy English squires, English peers, English bishops and English solicitors, was bound to blunt itself in drawing foreign models. Perhaps nobody could be so understanding of xenophobes but one who had a mild case of the same disease.

The Americans in Trollope's novels fall into three divisions of parody. They are unscrupulous adventurers, like Hamilton Fisker and Winifred Hurtle in *The Way We Live Now*, or grotesque, unsexed women who advocate radical causes, like the Vermont suffragette in *Is He Popenjoy?* and the "Republican Browning" in *He Knew He Was Right*, or pompous political windbags, waving the stars and stripes in the disgusted eyes of their English cousins, like the visiting legislator in *The American Senator* and Jonas Spalding in *He Knew He Was Right*. All in all, they are an unlovely crew, united by the common bond of a "strong nasal twang" and their creator's clumsy spite in the selection of their names: Ezekiel Boncassen, Olivia Fleabody, Wallachia Petrie, Elias Gotobed, Jackson Unthank. I suppose, in justice to Trollope, we should remember that the emancipated Yankee female and the boasting Yankee statesmen may have been as fair game for caricature in the eighteen-seventies as the exiled grand duke in the nineteen-twenties and the bearded Freudian in the fifties. One has only to turn the pages of James's *The Bostonians* to see that such types as Dr. Fleabody and Miss Petrie were as irritating to their compatriates as to the British, and the flavor of Senator Gotobed is preserved to this day in the gusty perorations of convention hall oratory. The exuberant self-confidence of a postwar America (resentful, too, of British confederate sympathies) was probably hard for anyone to bear.

But if we can forgive Trollope his caricatures, it is more difficult to forgive him his attempts to be fair. A parody is quite acceptable as a parody. We are amused when Jonas Spalding, who has declaimed in town halls at home that no English aristocrat can be fitting company for a Christian American citizen, takes up his best gloves and umbrella to call on the son of an earl. And we delight in Miss Petrie when she speaks to the same unfortunate nobleman of "that small speck on the earth's broad surface, of which you think so much, and which we call Great Britain," and tells him that all courtiers will be cut down "with the withered grasses and thrown into the oven." We hardly blame him for wondering if he can bring himself to marry the friend of such a woman. But when Trollope begins to make a case for the American who is parodied, when he begins to point out, as he does with Senator Gotobed, that the misguided legislator is not such a bad fellow after all, he tips his hand to reveal that, in his opinion, Gotobed is no parody at all, but a living, breathing American senator. And this, even after a century, I am inclined to resent.

For never was the smugness of the British middle class more evident than in the chapters where Trollope analyzes Senator Gotobed's gullibility about the wicked Goarly, who has poisoned the hounds. The thesis is simple. If you're a British gentleman, and there's a villain about, you can probably smell him out. Your nose, at any rate, will be your best detective. All of the characters in *The American Senator*, except the senator himself, instinctively sense that Goarly has been the culprit. Has he not objected to the hunt crossing his land? In the same way all the characters in *The Duke's Children* immediately know that Major Tifto has driven that nail into Prime Minister's hoof. And, indeed, it ultimately turns out that Goarly *has* been the poisoner and that the bogus major *has* crippled the noble steed. But Senator Gotobed, in his irritating Yankee fashion, insists that it is not fair to condemn a man for a crime because he objects to a hunt, and Trollope leans over backwards to do justice to his point of view. Indeed, he argues, Gotobed may well be right — in principle. Indeed, there may be things wrong in England, possibly very serious things. But what, basically, is the use of principle in crime detection when the good old nostrils of prejudice can pick out the guilty man nine times out of ten? "Goarly is a surly cuss who hates hunting; therefore Goarly is the culprit" may seem a harsh syllogism to Americans ignorant of English ways, but if it be an exact one, how is Goarly hurt?

There is one American character, however, against whom Trollope had no prejudice. Radiant, gay, courageous, unconventional yet untouched by all things base, the Yankee heroine, accompanied by dim, nasal parents with whom she seems to have no affinity, makes her appearance on the shores of an old, wise, startled Europe in the later novels of Trollope, as in the early ones of James. The latter was guardedly generous about the success of his British competitor in a field which he must have regarded as peculiarly his own:

> The American girl was destined sooner or later to make her entrance into British fiction, and Trollope's treatment of this complicated being is full of good humor and that fatherly indulgence, that almost motherly sympathy, which characterizes his attitude throughout toward the youthful feminine. He has not mastered all the springs of her delicate organism nor sounded all the mysteries of her conversation.

Caroline Spalding in *He Knew He Was Right* and Isabel Boncassen in *The Duke's Children* marry into the peerage with the author's rather grudging approval, but that they should receive even the grudging approval of so firm an admirer of Britain's class system speaks worlds for the charm of the American girls whom Trollope must have met. Caroline has some of the freshness and pertness of Daisy Miller whom she antedates by a decade. Charles Glascock is immediately intrigued by the easy way in which she mocks him when he asks about New York:

> "You wouldn't like it at all," said Carry; "because you are an aristocrat. I don't mean that it would be your fault."
>
> "Why should that prevent my liking it — even if I were an aristocrat?"
>
> "One half of the people would run after you, and the other half would run away from you."

And when she discovers her betrothed kissing Nora Crowley's hand the day before their wedding, she simply observes:

> "Tomorrow, Mr. Glascock, you will, I believe, be at liberty to kiss everybody; but today you should be more discreet."

But if Caroline can laugh at others, she is also capable of taking herself and her Americanism with a desperate seriousness. She is not in the least dazzled by Glascock's rank, but she is very much concerned at the prospect of being snubbed by his family and friends. I believe in her naïve exaggeration of the problems in store and in her proud resolution to break off with her lover, and I am sure that she would have had an ugly, humorless girl friend in whose wisdom she would have had a willful faith, but Wallachia Petrie is so overdrawn that I cannot quite credit Caroline's dependence on her. That, however, is a detail. When Caroline tries to warn Glascock off, she is superbly comic in her earnestness. There are delightful echoes of Wallachia's lectures in her efforts to explain to him the incompatibility of the old and new worlds and the hopelessness of their ever understanding each other.

> "You think it is impossible, Miss Spalding?"
> "I fear so. We are so terribly tender, and you are always pinching us on our most tender spot. And we never meet you without treading on your gouty toes."
> "I don't think my toes are gouty," said he.
> "I apologize to your own, individually, Mr. Glascock, but I must assert that nationally you are subject to the gout."

There is certainly no coyness in her attempt to rebuff him. She bears down on Glascock as hard as a woman can bear. When he tells her sharply that he should not like his wife to call him a fool, she advises him to marry an English wife — and be safe. Of course it is the very thing that hooks him, but Caroline never intends it so. As Nora Crowley says, Caroline will look like a peeress and bears her honors grandly, but they will never harden her.

Caroline, however, is only a countess when we take leave of her, and Trollope had greater honors in store for another American girl. Isabel Boncassen, twelve years later, is to be nothing less than premier duchess of England. But if an American is going to earn such a prize, the American must be worthy of it, and to be worthy of it she must be aware of what it is. The trouble with such awareness, at least in novels, is that even the smallest amount may seem too much. The difference between Isabel and Caroline is that Isabel loves the peerage and hopes (in the nicest way) to become a peeress. In true American fashion she announces her ambition in one of her first passages with Lord Silverbridge.

> "Do you ever dance with bank clerks?"
>
> "Oh, dear yes. At least I suppose so. I dance with whoever comes up. We haven't got lords in America, you know!"
>
> "You have got gentlemen?"
>
> "Plenty of them — but they are not so easily defined as lords. I do like lords."
>
> "Do you?"
>
> "Oh yes — and ladies — Countesses I mean and women of that sort."

She is stating the literal truth. The remarkable thing about the novel is that Trollope beams his approval on Isabel's ambition and also on that of Francis Tregear who is interested in marrying Lady Mary Palliser only if he can be assured of her money. As a hero (which he is of a subplot) he is probably the most mercenary of Victorian fiction. Now it may be true that the Duke of Omnium's rank is so exalted and his wealth so enormous that it is impossible for his children's suitors not to be affected by the prospect, but what makes the atmosphere of the novel so unpleasant is Trollope's evident feeling that it would be a kind of *lèse-majesté* for any young man or woman *not* to be affected. To love Silverbridge for himself, in other words, might be an act of black republicanism. How could anyone with proper British values fail to appreciate such social altitude?

Trollope himself discloses a veneration for his Duke of Omnium that smacks of the tweeny reading tabloid accounts of royal princesses. The Duke is the most high-minded gentleman in all of England. He can pay £70,000 of his son's gambling debts and regret only the bad company in which the sum was lost. He devotes himself to the driest kind of statistical work and becomes an indispensable Chancellor of the Exchequer and, ultimately, prime minister. But if he had been born in the Massachusetts Bay colony, he could not have enjoyed his money or his rank less. The world for him is all duty, no play. He will not even hunt, which in a lesser Trollope character would be a sign of villainy. Where his philosophy is peculiarly repellent is that he despises all the aspects of ducal existence that we might enjoy: the beautiful possessions, the country life, the great, crowded weekends, the glittering dinners, and to venerate all the aspects which we dislike: the narrow genealogical snobbery and the unceasing sense of personal superiority. There was "an inner feeling in his bosom as to his own family, his own name, his own children and his own personal self which was kept altogether apart from his grand political theories." When the Duke has finally been induced to give his consent to the marriage of his daughter to a brilliant young member of Parliament and of his son to the beautiful daughter of a potential American presidential candidate, he simply mutters that his third child will probably bring home a kitchen maid. Yet this is a man whom we are intended to like and admire!

Trollope's enthusiasm for the Duke spills over on Lord Silverbridge. The oldest son and heir of the pompous and snobbish Omnium is represented as a gullible scatterbrain whose virtues consist of a boyish candor and extreme good looks. He is sent down from Oxford; he loses money to obvious crooks; he changes his political convictions (such as they are) because he dislikes the head of his party and he shows, from beginning to end, little understanding of other humans. Yet our American heroine, who, left to herself, has considerable clarity of vision, is made to view Silverbridge through the author's rose-colored lenses:

> She had never seen anything like him before—so glorious in his beauty, so gentle in his manhood, so powerful and yet so little imperious, so great in

> condition and yet so little confident in his own greatness, so bolstered up with external advantages, and yet so little apt to trust anything but his own heart and his own voice.

I fancy, in reading this passage, that I can hear the American eagle squawk with discontent. Would a sharp-eyed Yankee like Isabel be quite so subjugated by such a nincompoop? But as I read on, I think I would rather have her taken in by his looks — as can happen to even a clever girl — than by his rank. What am I to think of Isabel after the following?

> She was glad he was what he was. She counted in their full value all his natural advantages. To be an English duchess!

Both she and her rival, Lady Mabel Grex, are intent upon becoming duchesses. The only difference is that Lady Mabel Grex, with an honesty as rare as it seems unnecessary, keeps reminding herself that she is not in love with Silverbridge. Perhaps the rewards in later Trollope go to the wishful thinkers. After all that he has made me swallow of the glories of a coronet and a bursting bank account, I gag when presented with Silverbridge's ideas of life with Isabel:

> He had thoughts of days to come, when everything would be settled, when he might sit close to her and call her pretty names, when he might in

> sweet familiarity tell her that she was a little Yankee and a fierce republican, and "chaff" her about the stars and stripes; and then, as he pictured the scene to himself in his imagination, she would lean upon him and would give him back his chaff, and would call him an aristocrat and would laugh at his titles.

I don't believe that Isabel is going to laugh very much at titles which will then be her own. I am very afraid that, unlike Caroline Spalding's, her honors may harden her. Of course, it is true that the decades which followed publication of *The Duke's Children* witnessed dozens of such alliances. One cannot accuse Trollope of exaggeration in assuming a craze for titles among American girls of the era. But one can resent his attributing it to the finest and best of them. Trollope is more denigrating with his compliments than with his sneers. I have very little to say in defense of Senator Gotobed or Wallachia Petrie. But I hate to see Daisy Miller turned into a gold digger.

James and Bourget

THE ARTIST AND THE CRANK

JAMES, writing to Charles Eliot Norton in 1892, speaks with great candor of his friend Paul Bourget. "Have you read any of his novels?" he asks. "If you haven't, *don't*." How this would have pained poor Bourget, who in the dedication of *Cruelle Énigme* had publicly praised the other's *rare et subtil talent!* Yet if we apply James's injunction to Bourget's "serious," as opposed to his "society," novels, it will save us much travail. For, indeed, they express a repellent point of view.

Consider the three most celebrated. *Le Disciple* is the fable of a young man, deeply read in determinist philosophy, who, for reasons somehow attributable to his liberal education, plots the seduction, in cold-blooded steps, of the noble girl who loves him. *Un Divorce* is a warning, equally dire, of the results to be anticipated from the severance of the marriage tie. The heroine's first husband may be a vice-ridden monster, she herself an angel of patience and her second spouse a model of civic virtue — it can make no difference. The outcome is disaster for all. And in *L'Étape* the same stern finger points to the dangers of a too rapid changing of one's class. An atheist professor, born of peasant stock, attempts to raise his children in Paris, away from the soil to which they belong. The result? His son becomes a forger and embezzler, his daughter the victim of a licentious aristocrat. It seems astonishing that such dismal extracts, expressing a social philosophy so appalling, should once have been excitedly discussed in French literary circles, but we tend to forget how much of the royalist "ultra" point of view survived in France sixty years ago. Bourget as a young man had been deeply exposed to the forces of reaction by the national humiliation of 1870 and the excesses of the Commune. The tendency so engendered grew steadily through the years to burst into a fine bloom during the Dreyfus trial. Mauriac relates that when Paléologue protested to Bourget that the issue at stake was not the reputation of the military but justice to the accused, the latter retorted contemptuously, "*Je me moque de la justice!*" After that, it is no surprise to learn that throughout a long lifetime, ending in 1935, he should never once have exercised his privilege of voting.

So far, so bad. But there was more to Bourget than just the reactionary. He was, by all accounts, a brilliant and stimulating person of deep cultivation, widely traveled, married to a wife, who, according to Edith Wharton, was "a being so rare, so full of delicate and secret vibrations" that she never knew by what happy accident she had penetrated her "voluntary invisibility." James described her as ministering to her husband like "a little quivering pathetic priestess on a bas-relief." He had his reservations about Bourget, the man, but none about Bourget, the conversationalist. The latter, "one of the very first of all talkers," was his pipe line into intellectual Paris.

More importantly, however, Bourget was not all his life obsessed with the idea of saving France. In his earlier years he was content to be a novelist and to amuse his reader. The books of this period, *Cruelle Énigme*, *Un Coeur de Femme*, *Mensonges* and *Un Crime d'Amour* were welcomed by a public sated with the dry monotony of a naturalist literature which had concentrated on the physical appearance of things to the exclusion of everything else. Bourget's deft handling of the psychology of love and jealousy came as a needed relief. I know it is the fashion today to downgrade these novels and to laud the graver note which Bourget struck in *Le Disciple*. There seems to be a feeling among certain critics that a writer ought to be given marks if he turns from duchesses to determinism, if, in their condescending term, he "matures." But the only question to me is: does he make determinism more entertaining? I agree with Louis Bertrand that the early period was Bourget's *jardin secret.*

We start in the Paris world of the upper bourgeoisie, but we rise on the social ladder as the novels progress, and from the upper rungs we view palazzos in Rome and villas on the Riviera. *Une Idylle Tragique* takes us to witness a Mediterranean race between three great steam yachts, an American millionaire's, a Russian grand duke's and an English peer's, on the last of which the Prince of Wales himself is a guest. But if the backgrounds are inclined to be lush, the details are still accurate and colorful, the characters vivid, the dialogue crisp and dramatic. The wealth of psychological detail gives to each story a rigorous, ordered framework, sometimes at the expense of reality, but artificial flowers have their claim to beauty. James, who in warning Norton off the novels had to admit their "remarkable qualities," saw the danger of his friend's excess of anticipatory analysis and of his tendency "to swim in the thick reflective element" in which he set his characters afloat. In his letter about *La Duchesse Bleue* he observes:

> Your love of intellectual daylight, absolutely your pursuit of complexities, is an injury to the patches of ambiguity and the abysses of shadow which really are the clothing — or much of it — of the *effects* that constitute the material of our trade. *Basta!*

Adultery is the central theme of this period of Bourget's work. Statesmen, bankers, titled idlers, fashionable artists and their wives are all engaged, in one way or another, knowingly or unknowingly, in playing the dangerous game. To the conscious players it is a completely absorbing occupation which taxes all their ingenuities. For in a Bourget world the astute psychologist has the advantage of being able to predict his victim's reactions and is thus assured of success if he only acts correctly. It is therefore worth his while to spend weeks or even months stalking his quarry. If he is a man, he may pose elaborately as a reformed roué (*Un Coeur de Femme*), calling on his victim throughout a whole season without once declaring himself in order to establish a solid new reputation. If a woman (*Mensonges*) she may go to equal lengths to appear as a loyal, faithful, misunderstood spouse seeking harmless recreation in picture galleries. But when success has been achieved — and it always is — the same procedure is observed by all characters.

Immediately, the man will rent and redecorate an apartment in a district unfrequented by the lady's acquaintance, with a sitting room so that the bed may not be observed, either before or after. When the lovers meet at parties in the great world, they murmur daytime assignations *chez nous*. The lady will dress, on the morning of a rendezvous, in clothes that are easy to remove without the assistance of her maid and proceed to the rented flat in a cab (never, of course, in her carriage). When the rites of love have been celebrated the couple will sip a glass of wine before returning to the more ordinary occupations of their day. In this brief interlude the lady may contemplate her satisfied lover in hazy rapture, if she happens to love him, or with an acid eye if her motive is merely to supplement her husband's inadequate income, or with a troubled conscience if she still has religious scruples. It may occur to her that she takes great risks for fleeting pleasures. It certainly occurs to the reader. For under the good manners of her polished world lurks the constant danger of violence. Sooner or later there will be a confrontation, between husband and lover, or lover and lover, and she will be disgraced, anathematized and spotted with blood. The end of a Bourget novel is like Gerôme's painting, *The Duel after the Ball*, with a dying Pierrot sinking into the arms of his seconds on an early snowy morning while his victorious opponent, also in costume, stalks off to a waiting fiacre. The Bourget heroine is a bewildered, defiant, hunted creature who snatches what pleasure she can in an oriental world of passionate, unreasonable men, knowing that she will one day be indicted and terribly punished for infidelities permissible to their sex but not to hers. What makes one increasingly uncomfortable is one's suspicion and ultimately one's certainty that the author feels her fate to be a just one. It is a point of view that may have received its sublimest expression in Shakespeare, but was not its lowest Jack the Ripper?

James was appalled at the erotic details of these early

novels. He would not allow that they were proper subjects for fiction. In a letter to Bourget about *Mensonges* he argues that the essential character of love-making lends itself more to action than to reflection, that the moment a novelist begins to "splash about" in it intellectually, it becomes unhealthy and unpleasant. He accuses Bourget of consecrating to Madame Moraines "and her underclothing" an imagination worthy of a greater cause. And for the sensitive young hero who attempts suicide when he discovers that his mistress, a married woman, is something less than an angel of purity, James has nothing but "*un coup de pied dans le derrière.*" That the world is full of such things is all the more reason for the novelist not to flood us with them.

James may have gone a bit far — at least in the eyes of a world of John O'Hara readers — but it was advice from which Bourget could have profited. For somewhere along the line, as happened with Dumas Fils, his denouncing side got out of hand. A modern John the Baptist, he turned his finger of scorn from Salomé to the world that had produced her. Society, in his later novels, has no more traditions and no more roots. A Jew like Hafner can rob his way to fortune and marry his daughter to a Roman prince. An octoroon can be the wife of a famous painter and move in the highest circles. And the morganatic wife of an Austrian archduke can receive her lover in the stateroom of an American yacht. If international society had taken on the worst features of the nations that composed it, the only hope for a Frenchman was to stay in his home, in his class and in his church. For the aging Bourget, the menace of the future must have seemed less Hitler or Stalin than Elsa Maxwell. Small wonder that his last years were depressed and his tales somber. He had allowed the crank to swallow the novelist.

Now James, on the other hand, though a man of far greater humaneness (he was on Zola's side in the trial), could be a bit of a crank himself. He deplored the absence in American life of such items of "high civilization" as a sovereign, a court, an aristocracy, old country houses, thatched cottages and ivied ruins; he hankered for "the luxuries and splendors of life," for "Old World drawing rooms with duskily moulded ceilings." One almost suspects that he considered the solace of the humble to lie in the contemplation of the elegance of their betters, for if, like Hyacinth Robinson, they were truly conscientious, they could take no part in the damaging of bric-à-brac that so often accompanies sudden upheavals in the social order. James's letters and travel books are spotted with nostalgia for a world of aristocratic order and tradition that must have appealed to Bourget. But a vital distinction exists. James wanted such a world as a painter might want a particular model, because he sought to recreate it. Its function was to supply him with *données* and his to turn them into beautiful tales. As long as he could reproduce and interpret, he had no need to *change* anything. He never had anything as vulgar as an axe to grind.

It is significant to note that despite all the literary chatter of the past twenty years about James as a moralist or philosopher or social commentator, there is not a phrase in all of his published notebooks to indicate that he ever had anything in mind in his writing but to translate little patches of anecdote in terms of his individual aesthetic. I know of no more illuminating study of the artistic process, though a layman's reaction might well be: "It *that* all it is?" The germ of James's initial idea is impossible to predict or explain; it simply comes. A dinner companion may be telling him a story or describing a family problem, and suddenly he knows that it is *his*. He jots it down later and proceeds to dramatize it, shifting the variables about in different combinations. Is it a daughter chained to her mother's sickbed? Can she escape? Does she? If she does, and flies to Europe, what will become of the mother? Is she cured? Does she rise from her chaise longue in hot pursuit? And might the daughter not then return, her eager parent at her heels? Might they not, pursued and pursuer, cross and recross the ocean indefinitely? "The scenic method," he writes, "is my absolute, my imperative, my *only* salvation." As the characters begin to move across the proscenium of his imagination, entering and exiting in different combinations, he communes with his director-intelligence in crooning phrases of passionate invocation:

> Ah, things swim before me, *caro mio*, and I only need to sit tight, to keep my place, and fix my eyes, to see them float past me in the current into which I can cast my little net and make my little haul.

Or:

> . . . the prospect clears and flushes, and my poor blest old Genius pats me so admirably and lovingly on the back that I turn, I screw round, and bend my lips to passionately, in my gratitude, kiss its hand.

Whatever one's reaction, one has certainly peeked into the mind of an artist at work. It may come as an anticlimax to some. They may prefer the more edifying picture of the author of *L'Étape* approaching his task of saving France. One sees Bourget, with that obsession of French novelists after Balzac to regard their scattered works as a unified *comédie humaine*, grimly considering which aspects of modern degeneration next to treat with his scalpel. The man who in 1885 had written that he and James, in talks about the novel, had finally agreed that all laws pertaining to it boiled down to the need of giving a personal impression of life had long been lost in the reformer and patriot. The older Bourget succeeded only in giving a personal impression of himself.

His nearest return to readable fiction was with *L'Émigré*, in which he drew a vivid and sympathetic portrait of an old marquis, possessed of a great name and chateau, prodigally dispensing his capital to keep up the standards of the *ancien régime* in 1906. The marquis passionately believes in the duty of the aristocracy to close ranks and preserve what is left of the old France for the day when the disillusioned new shall look again to her true leaders. He abhors all modern inventions, from the automobile to the telephone; he regards the officials of the Third Republic as so many Dantons and Marats, and he is prepared to break forever with his only son upon the latter's engagement to a woman whose sole demerit is her middle-class birth. But he also is a generous and trusting friend, a father to his tenants, a princely host, a man of absolute integrity and courage, a comic as well as a tragic character, in short, a magnificent anachronism. We sympathize with him, but never with his creator. It is easier to forgive a Marquis de Claviers-Grandchamp for tracing all the evils of his century to the fall of the Bastille than it is a Paul Bourget. And that is something which a novelist should never forget. Even his own prejudices can be put to work, but they must first be dramatized.

The Novel of Manners Today

MARQUAND AND O'HARA

HORTENSE CALISHER once told me that, as a writer, she envied me my family. It was her idea that the layers and layers of cousins, concentrated in Manhattan and belonging to a tribe that had done business there for a century and a half, should be grist for any novelist's mill. And so it might have been, a hundred years ago, in a world where family meant something broader than parents and children and where nepotism was a fact and not a bogey. But today, where it is considered rather pedantic to emphasize any relationship more distant than that of first cousins, the different branches of a large family have little more in common than what everyone has in common, and what is that for a novelist?

Perhaps I should state that I am not hankering after any good old days. I have no desire to return to a New

York where servants slept in unheated cubicles on the top of drafty brownstones, with an evening off every second week, and where W. A. Croffut, in his public eulogy of the Vanderbilt family, could describe the old Commodore as "puffed with divine greed." But every writer has two points of view about the society in which he lives: that of a citizen and that of an artist. The latter is concerned only with the suitability of society as material for his art. Just as a liberal journalist may secretly rejoice at the rise of a Senator McCarthy because of the opportunity which it affords him to write brilliant and scathing denunciations of demagogues, so will the eye of the novelist of manners light up at the first glimpse of social injustice. For his books must depend for their life blood on contrast and are bound to lose both significance and popularity in a classless society.

Such great social novelists of the last century as Balzac, Dickens and Trollope attempted nothing less than a reproduction of contemporary society. Even Jane Austen, who limited herself to a village, described in *Emma* a goodly portion of it. Yet, however crowded and variegated their novels, the writers of the century share a common denominator of clearly defined class feeling. Usually it is the author's feeling against the class immediately above him in actual life. Those prickly governesses of the Brontë sisters, those impecunious daughters of Jane Austen's country gentlemen, those rural young men in Balzac and Thackeray whose purses are too small for metropolitan pleasures, those hungry curates in Trollope, may all glare resentfully up the social ladder, but they also stare rather condescendingly down it. One wonders if Victorian fiction could ever have attained its bulk without keeping its nose so firmly buried in the rich trough of Victorian snobbishness.

It was not, of course, that the social barriers were impassable. The whole drama of Victorian fiction is precisely that they *were* passable. Where would its heroes and heroines be without its Darcys and Lady Catherine de Bourghs, its Lord Steynes and Dukes of Omnium, to get around? Can one imagine Jane Eyre or Julian Sorel or Emma Bovary without an upper class to resent or conquer or envy? But passing the barriers was always an event. If you made a fortune in the City and married a duke's daughter, everyone knew you were taking a great step. Travel between the social strata had not become the clanging escalator that it is today.

There was, however, more than snobbishness at the base of the nineteenth century novel of manners. There were all the things that go with snobbishness, or, rather, that go with the hierarchical society in which snobbishness is bred. There was fierce prejudice (or idealism, depending on the point of view); there was bigotry (or religiosity) and a passionate concern with the niceties of deportment and the chastity of women. The fiction of the era is peopled with fascinating extremists, magnificently logical and magnificently unjust, whose stubborn obsessions and murderous jealousies result in the most appalling catastrophes. Where would the English plot have been without the violently opposed marriage, or the French without the duel ? Say what one will about sentimentality and prolixity, it was still a pretty good show.

The public, anyway, loved it, and the public still does. It is a commonplace that the psychological novel, or the stream-of-consciousness novel, or the symbolic novel, has never enjoyed even a small fraction of the popularity of the novel of manners. The book clubs today clamor for a big meaty story about some phase of contemporary society, told from varied points of view and filled with graphic detail. Witness the sale of Allen Drury's study of the United States Senate. It is my simple thesis that the failure more generally to produce this kind of novel is not attributable to the decadence or escapism of mid-twentieth century writers, but rather to the increasingly classless nature of our society which does not lend itself to this kind of delineation. I do not mean by this that we are any duller than the Victorians, but simply that the most exciting and significant aspects of our civilization are no longer to be found in the distance and hostility between the social strata.

John P. Marquand engaged in the Balzacian task of drawing a picture of contemporary American society through a series of fictional biographies. We have a good tycoon, a bad tycoon, a general, a news commentator, a trust officer, a successful playwright, a Boston Brahmin of the old type and one of the new. Except for the Brahmins, the subjects are apt to be of middle class New England origin — often from a town called Clyde in Massachusetts — and their past hovers over their heads, even in the days of their triumph, like a miasma. They are never free of the sense of social distinctions bred into them in childhood. Afraid of condescending and afraid of being condescended to, they are haunted by the idea that they have not alighted on just the right rung of the social ladder. Into their make-up goes a strange mixture of ambition and humility, with some of the drive of the parvenu and some of the resignation of an old English servant. When I think of a Marquand novel I am apt to think of two characters, acquainted from boyhood, facing each other awkwardly over the gulf created by the success of one, as in *Women and Thomas Harrow*, when the local boy returns to buy the big house on the fashionable street and employs an old schoolmate to replant the garden.

> "Hello, Jack," Tom Harrow said.
>
> "Hello, Tom," Jack Dodd said. "You're looking good."
>
> There must have been some sort of reverse explanation of why he was pleased that Jack Dodd should call him Tom. He could never be wholly at ease with Jack Dodd or with other of his contempo-

raries there in town, when he could deal with people in any other place in the world adroitly, affably, and without the slightest sense of strain.

It is not a coincidence that the finest novel of a writer so obsessed with the problem of class consciousness should be concerned with the past. The late George Apley's dates are 1866 to 1933, and he is born at the summit of a formidable Boston pyramid of classes which would have provided Trollope with as rich material as Barsetshire. We are shown the warping of Apley's character by the forces of property and position, we see him lose his early struggle for independence and the Irish girl whom he wants to marry, and we see him settle down at last in defeat to a life of bird watching, civic duties and the arid satisfaction of denouncing a new world. Yet for all his flag waving and for all his bitter prejudices, Apley remains a man of courage and a man of heart. His defeat is brought about by a wholly sincere veneration for the opposing forces. To have married Mary Monahan would have cost him the esteem of every human being whom he has been brought up to admire and disqualified him for the position of leadership that he believes it his duty to take up. The defeat of such a man holding to such a creed is not tragic, but it is pathetic, and pathos has a bigger place than tragedy in the study of manners.

H. M. Pulham, Esquire proves that the passing of a single generation has stripped the conflict of its pathos.

Why should Harry Pulham (who might be Apley's son), a war hero, working in an advertising agency in New York, not marry Marvin Miles? His family might have frowned and criticized her dress and speech, but they would have come around soon enough. Such marriages were everyday affairs in the twenties, even in Boston. Pulham himself recognizes the change in the times when he assesses the social opportunities which his friend, Bill King, has passed up:

> Bill would actually have got on very well at Harvard, I think, if he had cared about trying. It was true that he did not have any connections, but if he had gone out for something besides the Dramatic Club, such as the Lampoon, or even the Crimson, and if he had bothered with the people to whom I had introduced him and who usually liked him, he would very possibly have made a Club.

We see what has happened. Bill King doesn't *want* a club, and Marvin Miles doesn't want Pulham. The shoe is now on the other foot. The trouble is that if Marvin doesn't want him, the reader isn't going to want him very much, either, for Marvin is a shrewd girl. Pulham's problem is not, like Apley's, that he is caught in the vise of a social system, but that he is totally lacking in humor and imagination. It is a bit difficult to sympathize with or even to believe in a decorated war hero who is afraid to ask the family butler for an extra glass and so disclose to the world below stairs that the woman he loves wants a drink before dinner.

After *Pulham* Marquand was permanently stuck with the problem of creating heroes who had to be strongly influenced by less and less influential environments and who at the same time would not strike his readers as Casper Milquetoasts. He solved it partially with the gentleman hero of the suburbs, a kind, earnest patient man of an absolute but rather wearisome integrity, a faithful husband and adoring father, who plods through a dull life in a sleepwalking fashion, prodded by a nervous, suspicious wife who has invested her emotional being in local standards of success and is terrified that her house of cards will fall if she allows her husband, even in joke, to question the least of her adopted values. Charles Gray in *Point of No Return* and Bob Tasmin in *B. F.'s Daughter* both fail with their first loves because they don't push hard enough, thus perhaps deserving the fate of being pushed about by their second. A few words uttered or held back might have turned the scales in Tasmin's relationship with Polly Fulton. Yet he moodily blames his ineptitude on his inheritance:

> I've always been a goddam gentleman, and I've always been afraid not to be one. Let's put it on my tombstone. That's my whole obituary.

In the later novels the function of each hero's elaborately described background becomes even fuzzier.

What does that drugstore in Vermont have to do with Melville Goodwin's wanting to be a soldier? And how does Willis Wayde pick up the habit of sentimentalizing his motives and calling everything "lovely" in a bleak Yankee community like Clyde? Marquand seems to be tracing Willis' hunger for success to his family's move into the garden cottage on the great estate of the aristocratic Harcourts, a thoroughly Victorian situation. Bess Harcourt is as haughty as Pip's Estella, and poor Willis achieves his financial goal only to have her fling in his teeth a bitter Victorian epithet: "Get out of my way, Uriah Heep!" The moral seems to be that to such as Willis, the world of the fine old Harcourts, with its traditions of loyalty and integrity, will be forever closed. To such as Willis, yes. But why? Not because of his social ambition or even because of his business ruthlessness, but simply because of his drooling sanctimoniousness. If he had faced Bess Harcourt boldly, like a John O'Hara hero, and flung in *her* teeth that he was closing down the Harcourt mills because they didn't pay, she would have rewarded him as O'Hara ladies reward such heroes. What she really condemns him for (and who wouldn't?) is that he reads the Harvard Classics fifteen minutes a day and boasts about it.

My favorite of the novels, after *The Late George Apley*, is *Point of No Return*, perhaps because it dramatizes just the point that I have been trying to make, that the paralyzing effect of a class-conscious background is largely illusory. Charles Gray can only be liberated from Clyde by returning there and finding that Jessica Lovell is about to save herself from middle-aged spinsterhood by marrying Jackie Mason, who was born further down the social ladder than Charles himself. The poor old past is now revealed to him in all its smallness and sterility, as sad and foolish as Jessica's neurotic, deluded father who once told Charles that money made on the stock market was not the same as inherited money. So Charles goes back to New York and the Stuyvesant Bank, strengthened in the discovery that his youth was dominated by puppets, and finds that the promotion of which he has despaired has been assured him all along, that his rival for the bank vice-presidency has been as illusory as Clyde. His trip has had the effect of a psychoanalysis. But when the function of a character's background is only his misconception of it, the novel of manners has become a psychological novel.

I do not wish the reader to assume that I think we have attained the classless society. I am aware of the plight of Negroes in the South and of the terrible differences that still exist between rich and poor in our large cities. But every sociologist comments on our enormous suburban white-collar population and its habit of classifying the different strata of which it is composed by such artificial standards as number of automobiles or television sets. I do not deny that people can care passionately for such things or that their caring is a proper subject for a novelist, but it is thinner material than what the Victorian writers had to deal with. Today snobbishness is more between groups than classes, more between cliques than between rich and poor. Surely the resentment aroused is of a different degree. Surely there is a difference between the feelings of the man who has not been asked to dinner and those of the man who has been thrown down the front stairs. What I find out of proportion in the novels of John O'Hara is the significance which he attaches to the former.

In the strange, angry world that he describes, the characters behave with a uniform violence, speak with a uniform crudeness and make no appreciable effort to control lusts which they regard as ungovernable. The most casual meeting between a major and minor character will result either in an ugly flare-up or a sexual connection, or both. It is impossible for an O'Hara hero to order a meal in a restaurant or to take a taxi ride without having a brusque interchange with the waiter or driver. Even the characters from whom one might expect some degree of reticence — the rich dowagers, for example — will discuss sex on the frankest basis with the first person to bring the subject up. And in Gibbsville or Fort Penn the first person to bring it up is the first person one meets. A great deal is said about each character's exact social position, perhaps because it is so difficult to determine it from his habits and conversation. Everyone, apparently, does *everything*, and everyone knows that everyone else is doing it. But that does not mean that the shibboleths of an older society are dead. Far from it. The code of an earlier culture, though only dimly remembered, is superstitiously venerated. O'Hara's men and women dance around the Victorian traditions of class distinction and sexual restraint like savages around a cross left by murdered missionaries and now adorned with shrunken heads. The hatred of the immigrant who coughed his lungs out in a coal mine is kept alive in the hatred of the rich Irishman who can't get into the Lantenengo Country Club. And although the O'Hara hero knows that sexual liberty is now the rule, he clings to a dusky little hope that the magic of the marriage vow will somehow safeguard his spouse. Thus Robert Millhouser in *Ourselves to Know*, a man versed in the ways of prostitutes, who has married a nymphomaniac half his age with full notice of her vicious propensities, shoots her dead without a qualm when he discovers that she has been unfaithful to him.

From time to time there emerges from the jungle a superman or superwoman, the darling of the author, to dominate the scene, such as Grace Caldwell Tate in *A Rage to Live* and Alfred Eaton in *From the Terrace*. They differ from their contemporaries in that they have a little more of everything — more sex appeal, more brains, more money, more social position. But, above all, they have more defiance. They look the universe in the eye and spit. They are defeated in the end of their chronicles, but only by accumulated envy; they have not been able to learn that the other beasts in the jungle cannot endure the sight of so many advantages. Grace Tate might have been able to live in Fort Penn with a husband, but as a beautiful widow she is hounded out of town as an unmated lioness is hounded out of the pride by the others of her sex. And Alfred Eaton, for all his brilliant capabilities, is condemned to a life of idleness because he is too plain spoken. The *hubris* of O'Hara's superpeople is not that they have offended the gods. They have offended the grubby little people who share their faults but resent their success.

If O'Hara were consciously trying to describe the chaos of a society where each individual flouts the moral code, yet applies it with brutal bigotry to his neighbor, and where the inhabitants of every town play at being masters and serfs like boys and girls in a school play dressed up in wigs and hoops, he might be a more important novelist than he is. Surely it is a damning picture of the contemporary world. But my complaint is that what he seems to be doing, underneath all the violence and bluster, is to be writing an old-fashioned novel of manners where the most important item about any character is the social niche in which he was born. Each hero must start the race of life with a particular ribbon pinned to his lapel, and he will never be able to take it off, whether he be proud of it or ashamed. To O'Hara, in other words, it really seems to matter if he belongs or does not belong to the Lantenengo Country Club.

If background is everything, background must be described in detail, and O'Hara's descriptions amount almost to inventories. A friend of mine, who was brought up in a Pennsylvania town similar to Gibbsville, assures me that these descriptions are remarkably accurate. But I question their significance. When I learn that Mary Eaton's father wore "pince-nez spectacles with small lenses, a blue and white polka dot bow-tie and a Tau Beta Pi key on his watch chain," that his "tan kid oxfords were polished and he had on black silk socks with a thin white stripe," I do not immediately realize that he is half business man, half professor. I can think of too many lawyers and judges and doctors who might be guilty of the same combination. Nor do I really see the difference in Fort Penn between those who say "The Tates" and those who say "Sidney and Grace." Nor do I really believe that Mary Eaton's Rowland blood would make her "automatically acceptable" to anybody. When Grace Tate tells Roger Bannon that it would take her a lifetime to explain the difference between him and the men at the Fort Penn Club, I wonder if at the end of the lifetime he would know. But she teaches him more than she thinks with a single word:

> "A lady? What do you know about a lady? Where would you ever learn about a lady? Have

you ever seen one? You contemptible son of a bitch, you wouldn't know a lady if you saw one."

"Yes, I would. You're a lady, and probably you're acting like one."

"Oh, balls."

When he takes for his hero a Gibbsville aristocrat of the old school, O'Hara, like Marquand with George Apley, writes his most successful novel of manners. Joe Chapin, in *Ten North Frederick*, is a man who has been brought up with high ideals (though this is largely blamed on a passionately possessive mother), and he is unique among O'Hara characters in that he seeks to live according to his own somewhat fuzzy conception of the old moral code. He is faithful to his wife, conscientious and high-minded in the practice of law and active in civic affairs. The tragic flaw in his character is his irrational belief that he is destined to become the President of the United States. Many men have been so obsessed but few can have suffered from Joe's peculiar delusion that he could attain his objective by the simple expedient of attending meetings of bar associations. The other characters are puzzled as to what Joe is up to, and, indeed, it takes all the genius of Mike Slattery to guess it from the nature of Joe's activity. When Joe, in his late fifties, finally decides that the time is ripe to throw his hat in the ring, he offers Mike a hundred thousand dollars for the nomination of lieutenant-governor. Mike quietly pockets the money for the party, and Joe is left to drink himself to death. It is difficult to be sympathetic with a man so deluded, and it is not clear that Joe's ideals at the end are any higher than Mike Slattery's, but the contrast between the two men is always interesting. We see Joe against a background of privilege and Mike against its opposite; we see the even greater disparity between their wives; we see Joe fumble, outmaneuvered, and fall into the clutches of his wily and contemptuously pitying opponent, and we learn more about the forces of society that has placed the two in conflict than in a whole volume about polka-dot ties and fraternity pins.

When I turn, on the other hand, to the defeat of Julian English in *Appointment in Samarra*, I can understand it only in terms of a compulsion to suicide. Taken as such, the novel is certainly a powerful description of self-destruction, possibly one of the most powerful ever written. But again I am troubled with the nagging suspicion that this may not be what the author intends. Is Julian meant to be destroyed by himself or by Gibbsville? Does his instinct to antagonize lead him surely to the most dangerous persons, or is their envy of his looks, his breeding, his easy manner and apparent success what makes them hunt him down? Had Julian lived elsewhere than in Gibbsville, that lumberyard of chips on the shoulder, would he have survived? But I suppose such speculations are idle. Julian belongs to Gibbsville, and it is never difficult to find enough hate in Gibbsville with which to destroy oneself. From one end of town to the other the populace fairly throbs with hurt feelings. Al Grecco provides its motto as he drives through Lantenengo Street early Christmas morning and lowers the car window to shout out at the darkened homes:

"Merry Christmas, you stuck-up bastards! Merry Christmas from Al Grecco!"

Perhaps it is the motto of O'Hara himself and of the contemporary novel of manners.

James and the Russian Novelists

JAMES usually spoke of Tolstoy in terms of guarded respect. His attitude was like that of Delacroix, who said to his students as they passed Ingres' Odalisque in the Louvre: *Messieurs, le châpeau dans la main, mais les yeux fixés à terre.* Neither Tolstoy nor Dostoyevsky was very much to his taste, and he regarded their effect on other writers as little short of disastrous. Turgenev, on the other hand, he loved and admired, both as a friend and a writer, but then Turgenev was a sort of Russian Henry James, an expatriate who cultivated the French novelists and was regarded as an equal by Flaubert himself. His concern, like James's, was with the fine details of craftsmanship; he was, in the latter's phrase, the novelist's novelist, "an artistic influence extraordinarily valuable and ineradicably established." Too many of Turgenev's rivals, James complained, "appear to hold us in compari son by violent means, and introduce us in comparison to vulgar things."

Did he mean to include Tolstoy among these rivals? It seems likely. For observe how he contrasts him with Turgenev:

> The perusal of Tolstoy — a wonderful mass of life — is an immense event, a kind of splendid accident, for each of us: his name represents nevertheless no such eternal spell of method, no such quiet irresistibility of presentation, as shines, close to us and lighting our possible steps, in that of his precursor. Tolstoy is a reflector as vast as a natural lake; a monster harnessed to his great subject — all human life! — as an elephant might be harnessed, for purposes of traction, not to a carriage, but to a coach house. His own case is prodigious, but his example for others dire: disciples not elephantine he can only mislead and betray.

The compliment, if one was intended, fades under the words "monster" and "elephant." Later James became more candid. When Hugh Walpole wrote to ask him if he did not feel that Dostoyevsky's "mad jumble that flings things down in a heap" was nearer truth than the "picking and composing" of Stevenson, James seized the occasion to state his credo in organ tones:

> Form alone *takes*, and holds and preserves, substance — saves it from the welter of helpless ver-

> biage that we swim in as in a sea of tasteless tepid pudding, and that makes one ashamed of an art capable of such degradations. Tolstoy and Dostoyevsky are fluid pudding, though not tasteless, because the amount of their own minds and souls in solution in the broth gives it savour and flavour, thanks to the strong, rank quality of their genius and their experience. But there are all sorts of things to be said of them, and in particular that we see how great a vice is their lack of composition, their defiance of economy and architecture, directly they are emulated and imitated; *then*, as subjects of emulation, models, they quite give themselves away.

Leon Edel maintains that the now famous term "fluid pudding" has been misunderstood and that James meant so to characterize the novels of the two Russian authors only insofar as they are used as models. But I question this. A fluid pudding is a fluid pudding, whether one eats it or paints it. James evidently considered the process of imitation as a peculiarly revealing one, for it is precisely here, in his opinion, that Tolstoy and Dostoyevsky "quite give themselves away" i.e., expose their essential fluidity. But surely these imitators, whoever they were, failed because they saw only formlessness where there was form, just as so many Jamesian imitators have seen only form where there was substance. If we are to rate novelists by the efforts of those who copy them, James will fare quite as badly as Tolstoy or Dostoyevsky.

A year later James wrote another letter to Walpole in which he dropped the last pretense of admiration for Tolstoy. If his term "fluid pudding" has been misunderstood, surely there is no misunderstanding the following:

> I have been reading over Tolstoy's interminable *Peace and War*, and am struck with the fact that I now protest as much as I admire. He doesn't *do* to read over, and that exactly is the answer to those who idiotically proclaim the impunity of such formless shape, such flopping looseness and such a denial of composition, selection and style. He has a mighty fund of life, but the *waste*, and the ugliness and vice of waste, the vice of a not finer *doing* are sickening. For me he makes "composition" throne, by contrast, in effulgent lustre!

It was unfortunate that Walpole should have been the person to invite James to consider the Russians. For he did it in such a way as to raise the master's ire against a straw man; he must have known perfectly well that to ask a lover of Stevenson to admire a "mad jumble" was like asking the Pope to admire Luther. He wanted a strong reaction, and he got it. James's explosion has provided a perfect text for extremists to fight over through the years. On one side we can line up all who excuse their clumsy craftsmanship by greatness of purpose, their fudged details by the scope of their panorama, those who profess to deal in raw chunks of life salted with "compassion." On the other we can line up those attenuated scribblers who seek with polished phrases to conceal that they have nothing to write about. It is all great fun, and everybody gets very heated, but we must remember that it is only a parlor game. It has nothing to do with literature, and it has nothing to do with art.

For James's impatience with the formlessness that he unfairly attributed to the Russian novelists leads him to make a false distinction between a work of art and a "mass of life." Tolstoy, according to him, is not an artist but a "reflector of life." Tolstoy and Dostoyevsky fail in composition, but are saved by the "strong, rank quality of their genius and their experience." Now this, I submit, is meaningless. Tolstoy could only reflect life through his art. If life is reflected, it is because art succeeds, and if art succeeds, it is because the form is right. Life is only a subject; it cannot rub off onto a book any more than a bowl of fruit can rub off onto a canvas. There is only one process for James as for Tolstoy, and that process is art. There they fail or there they succeed. "Life" will not help either in the least bit.

Because *War and Peace* is a long book and has many characters, it has been said to "sprawl." Yet actually it is unified by the Napoleonic invasion of Russia which directly affects the outward and inner life of every character. It is true that Tolstoy continually shifts the point of view from character to character, but how else could he succeed in re-creating a war? James can confine *The*

Ambassadors to Strether's point of view because Strether's point of view is the subject of the novel, but if he had set himself Tolstoy's job, he would have needed not one, but a hundred pairs of eyes. In any event, I agree with E. M. Forster that the question of the point of view is one more interesting to writers than readers. It was vital to the construction of James's novels, but it is not vital to that of all others.

To me there is "flopping looseness" in *War and Peace* only in Tolstoy's essays on military and historical theory. I find these as intrusive and boring as commercials in a television play, but they are easily skipped, so long as one is careful not to skip with them the chapters dealing with the personalities of the war leaders and the battle scenes, which are of the essence of Tolstoy's scheme. The pictures of Kutuzov at the front and of Napoleon watching the drowning of the overeager cavalry, of the battlefield of Borodino and of the burning of Moscow, give us the historical perspective against which the individuals must be seen. The form of the novel is the same that was used by Margaret Mitchell in *Gone With the Wind:* the principal character, Armageddon, unites the other characters and changes their lives. But form can be obvious and still be form. And is there a better fictional device for a war?

It is fashionable to describe *War and Peace* as a great, crowded canvas, and to think of Tolstoy as daubing at it with broad strokes. But the more I look at it, the more I am astonished (outside of the essay sections) at the amount of meticulous craftsmanship involved. As Max Reinhardt was able to create the illusion of a vast army with a few soldiers, so does Tolstoy create a mighty conflict with a whiff of smoke, a bit of snow and a handful of aristocrats from Russian court society. Think of our own war novelists and how carefully they delineate the assorted backgrounds of the soldiers of a squadron. Think of those flashbacks that show the lieutenant at Groton and the Negro private in an overcrowded Southern school. Imagine Norman Mailer limited in *The Naked and the Dead* to the Lowells and Cabots of Boston! Yet Tolstoy's characters are not only from the same social milieu; they are almost all related to each other. I suppose it is true that the great landlords and serf owners of an absolute monarchy were more representative of their nation than capitalists are of a democracy, but even so, Tolstoy is telling the story of Russia's agony from the viewpoint of a very tiny class of sufferers. What he understands is that if a human being is described completely, his class makes little difference. He becomes a human being on the printed page, and other humans, of whatever class, can recognize themselves in his portrait. The lesson of Tolstoy is precisely how little of life, not how much, the artist needs.

The only moral classifications into which Tolstoy divides his characters are those of serious and nonserious. If one is trivial-minded about the great questions of life, if one is bent on playing games, like Pierre's first wife, one is condemned. But as long as one cares about one's role in the universe, then, regardless of one's ineffectiveness, all is forgiven. Pierre, for example, makes a mess of everything that he touches, his estates, his marriage, even his social career. When war comes, he wanders, a useless civilian, about the battlefield at Borodino like a sleepwalker, concerned only with his own doubts about the purpose of life. He is arrested by the French in Moscow and suffers great hardships, but he still accomplishes nothing. Nobody but himself is helped by his agony. Prince André, on the other hand, looks after his serfs conscientiously, manages his estates economically and is a brilliant officer in the war. Yet there is no feeling in the novel that André is a "better" man than Pierre. They are both serious men and, as such, appreciate and understand each other. That one is effectively and the other ineffectively good is a mere detail. What concern has God with such details?

In *Anna Karenina* I find only Levin's agricultural theories "floppingly loose." They are as irrelevant to the story as the historical asides in *War and Peace*, and much more difficult to skip, being more deeply imbedded in the plot. But a graver fault in the structure of the novel is Tolstoy's failure to prepare us for Anna's adultery. We meet her first as a charming and deeply understanding sister-in-law who, by consummate tact, saves her brother's crumbling marriage, but we pass with a dizzy speed over the year which elapses between her meeting

Vronsky and her succumbing to him. We grasp Anna's character at last — or a good deal of it — but the hole in this part of the book is never quite filled. We never know why such a woman should have married a man like her husband or why, having done so, she should have been unfaithful to him. But aside from being occasionally bored by Levin and occasionally confused by the early Anna, I find no other looseness in the novel. It is like a well-organized English novel of its period: it has two plots, constantly interwoven and always in dramatic contrast, and in the end married love brings happiness and adultery despair. Even James could not have said that it contained the vice of waste.

Tolstoy liked to accomplish a great many obvious as well as a great many subtle things, and he was not afraid of old and well-worn formulas. What he needed for war was a burning capital and what he needed for a drama of love was a married and an unmarried couple. He never hesitated to hammer in his contrasts with heavy strokes. On the side of Kitty and Levin and lawful love are the rolling acres of a well-managed farm, and Moscow, no longer the capital, but still the center of the oldest, truest Russian values. On the side of Anna and Vronsky and illicit passion are the superficial court society of St. Petersburg and a motley pile of borrowed notions from Paris and London. The great columns of the two plots stand up before us, massive, conventional, imposing and trite, but on closer examination we find that the bas-reliefs that gird them have been carved with the greatest delicacy and skill. Whatever assumptions we make as we go along, we will find that we must qualify, until we begin to wonder if the two columns are twins or opposites.

Levin and Kitty, for example, may be depicted as the young couple on whose love we may properly smile, but in contrast to Anna and Vronsky they are frequently ridiculous. Levin is absurdly and irrationally jealous, and his nervousness on the birth of his child seems almost a caricature of the traditionally nervous father. He is violent, rude and ill-tempered, and Kitty is excitable and possessive. It is true that Tolstoy obviously likes Levin and considers his faults as rather lovably Russian, but he is careful at the same time to show us that the other characters consider him a bull in a china shop. Vronsky, on the other hand, leads a St. Petersburg society life of which his creator disapproves to such an extent that it has become traditional to regard him as a shallow gadabout who is unworthy of the passion that he has inspired in Anna. But consider him more closely. Vronsky may be irresponsible in seducing Anna, but after that he behaves with the greatest possible style. He is never unfaithful to her, never deserts her, always tries to spare her pain, does everything he can to legalize their relationship and even attempts suicide when none of his plans for her happiness work out. There are moments in the book when he and Anna seem a couple unjustly condemned by a censorious and hypocritical society, while

Kitty and Levin seem like spoiled youngsters who cannot find happiness in a veritable flood of good fortune.

For Tolstoy is not really condemning Anna, any more than he is praising Kitty. Anna is, indeed, the more high-minded of the two. He is rather proving that for women of their background and position (Levin's brother's mistress is quite happy as such), cohabitation outside of marriage is impossible. Kitty and Anna are both intensely female in their possessiveness. Levin feels, when Kitty wishes to accompany him to his brother's deathbed, that it is intolerable to be so shackled. Yet she comes and is a great help. Within the framework of a happy marriage such matters can always be adjusted. Kitty becomes absorbed in her babies, and Levin can then attend all the agricultural conventions that he wants. But no such adjustment is possible for Anna. She destroys her life with Vronsky by her mad jealousy and her need to be with him every moment. Anna turns into a kind of monster, making scenes over everything, crazed by the thought that her lover should have any life or interest outside the dull and lonely house where she rants at him. Vronsky is a model of patience and restraint, but he is helpless to arrest her insane course of self-destruction. Anna has been idle and restless in St. Petersburg society, but she is utterly shattered when its doors are closed to her but not to him. It is ridiculous; it is pathetic; it is nineteenth century but it is very feminine. Kitty would have been just as bad.

James in the letters to Walpole deals specifically with

Tolstoy, but Dostoyevsky is included at least by implication. Certainly James does nothing to rebut Walpole's assertion that the author of *Crime and Punishment* created his effects by "flinging things down in heaps." It is illuminating and also rather pathetic to contrast Walpole's fanciful picture with the actual one of Dostoyevsky, impoverished and epileptic, at work in Dresden on the manuscript of *The Idiot*. His notebooks show eight different proposed treatments of the central theme, and even when he had settled on the outline, the execution was agonizingly slow. He wrote to the poet Maykov:

> All this time I literally worked day and night in spite of my fits. But, alas, I notice with despair that for some reason I am not able to work as quickly as I did a short while ago. I crawl like a crab, and then I begin to count the sheets — three and a half or four in a whole month. This is terrible, and I don't know what will happen to me.

Surely the confusion that Walpole finds on the surface of the novels results from the magnitude of the author's task rather than from a failure in artistry. For, as is now commonly recognized, Dostoyevsky wanted to show man not only in relation to his fellow creatures but in his relation to God. Most of nineteenth century fiction was concerned with character; Dostoyevsky was concerned with soul. His subject required a new dimension and an immense amount of planning. It seems to me that even a cursory review of his books shows a love of craftsmanship as deep as that of James himself.

Dostoyevsky uses three principal techniques in the construction of his novels. The first is the dialogue, or general conversation, usually at a social gathering, where the characters argue with each other about themselves, social conditions in Russia, liberalism and religion. The talks are marked by irrelevancies, low comedy, testiness, self-pity and sudden violent fits of temper. Just when the action seems about to take a step forward, someone inevitably enters or changes the subject to arrest it, so that these sections of the novels have some of the static, frustrating quality of Ivy Compton-Burnett's dialogues. But the comedy, or at times farce, is always hilarious; the lies and antics of General Ivolgin and of old Karamazov have a Falstaffian richness. Farce and tragedy stand up boldly side by side in Dostoyevsky; together they make up the dreamlike quality of a mortal existence where we are separated from God.

The author, however, realizes that he cannot tell the whole story by such discussions, and at regular intervals he interrupts, with a firm editorial hand, to move his plot forward or to fill in the biographies of his characters. In these parts he is smooth, sharply analytical and brilliant. The passages in *The Idiot* that describe Madame Yepanchin's concern about her unmarried daughters are as vivid and clever as any of their counterparts in Jane Austen. Sometimes Dostoyevsky uses his editorial hand to tell a seemingly irrelevant story or legend like the famous "Grand Inquisitor" in *The Brothers Karamazov.* Certainly it absorbs us to a point where we forget the very novel of which it is a part. But as soon as we return to Ivan who has related it, we realize that it is the perfect parable of his own agnosticism, and the parable and Ivan are henceforth inseparable in our minds.

Finally, Dostoyevsky uses the method of dramatic, violent scenes that illuminate the dusky landscape with a sudden shocking light. He may use them as preludes, to foreshadow what is going to happen, or as crises, to explain what already has. In *The Brothers Karamazov* the great scene where the father and sons go to the monastery contains in it the germs of everything that happens afterward, whereas the scene in *The Idiot* where Nastasya, at her birthday party, elopes with Rogozhin, gives us the final key to a character who has hitherto baffled us. It is only when we read such a scene that we realize to the full how necessary the previous chapters have been.

What in all of this becomes of James's "point of view"? It is lost, of course. But it was vital for Dostoyevsky, in his psychic probing, to be able to move in and out of the mind of each of his characters, to substitute himself as narrator or as observer, or even to have the characters create other observers by telling stories. In the massive job that he set for himself he needed every trick in the novelist's bag, and he used them all. To have limited him to one would have been like limiting a playwright to the classic unities. Racine was content to contain his action to a single day and place, but what would have become of Shakespeare? I cannot imagine two novels more different than *The Brothers Karamazov* and *The Ambassadors*, nor can I imagine two novels more admirable. It is idle to choose between them, for one always has both.

Crisis in Newport — August, 1857

WITH PREVIOUSLY UNPUBLISHED EXTRACTS FROM THE DIARY OF GEORGE TEMPLETON STRONG

FEW INDIVIDUALS appear more frequently in the four million words of the diary of George Templeton Strong, the Pepys of nineteenth century New York, than his cousin "Charley." Charles E. Strong, four years younger than the diarist and a graduate of Amherst, entered the Wall Street law firm of Bidwell & Strong in 1843 when he was nineteen and practiced there until his death fifty-four years later. At that time he was senior partner and the firm had become Strong & Cadwalader (now Cadwalader, Wickersham & Taft). Like any diarist dealing with his daily intimates George never clearly describes Charley, and we have to look back at him from the memoir of a younger partner, Henry W. Taft, written as late as 1938, to see him as a "genial, benevolent, sympathetic, elderly gentleman," who may never have tried a case, but who for generations was the trusted adviser to "many of the wealthiest families of the city." It is not too easy to reconstruct the younger Charley from this, but we learn from the diary that he was a loyal friend and popular man about town, and from an early photograph, that he had wavy blond hair and a small mustache, and could strike a rather dashing pose with a Prince Albert and cane. One suspects that Charley was not without his reserve of charm. Certainly he was a less complicated man than his diarist cousin. George, introspective and nervous, subject to moods of melancholia despite a rather Dickensian sense of humor, was an earnest and sincere Victorian who thought little enough of his age and less of himself, but who was desperately determined to make the best of both. If his prejudices were violent, his instincts were good; he may have disliked the Irish, the English and the South, but he also detested municipal corruption and colonialism, and he abhorred slavery. He had a fondness for reading, an enthusiasm for personalities, a love of music and a passion for recording everyone and everything in the pages of his voluminous diary. Though obviously a competent practitioner, he never cared for the law as Charley did; he did not have the latter's patience for plugging away at the details of wills and deeds. It is easy to imagine that Charley provided a needed balance to his more volatile cousin, a steadying influence at home and in the office. "There are not many people for whose sickness or health I care a great deal," George notes when his cousin is ill, "and Charley is among the more precious of those few."

It is with great excitement, therefore, that George, in 1850, records Charley's engagement, after a feverish courtship, to Eleanor Fearing, charming, popular and rich, the catch, indeed, of the New York and Newport social seasons. George himself had been married only two years before, and he and his wife (Ellen Ruggles) clucked benevolently over the younger couple. "It is delicious to be in the society of so happy a man as Charley," he writes, "so happy and so hopeful and so outrageously in love." When Eleanor and Charley meet at George's, their presence gives his house "a kind of domestic consecration." In fact, he is quite carried away as his mind roams over the world to think of all the other happy couples "in gay capitals and secluded little towns, in stately old ancestral homes and around humble fire-sides, everywhere, from the long resounding fjords of the North to the bright shores of the Mediterranean." His heart overflows:

> How many thousands of capital fellows as happy as Charley, and each with the same sufficient reason, and all with the same blue sky and bright stars looking quietly down on their happiness. Think of the thousands of beautiful girls, too, blonde and brunette of every shade, simple-hearted little rusticities not dressed in the best taste, and radiant,

> highbred beauties of every degree, whose little hands are trembling and whose little heads are swimming *tonight,* as they think of the mighty event of the last week and of the announcements and congratulations of tomorrow.

Let it not be deduced that George's own bride was any "simple-hearted little rusticity," or that her dresses were not in the best taste. Ellen Strong was a daughter of Samuel B. Ruggles, the financier. It was simply that her husband had an obsession for the diminutive in all affectionate descriptions of the opposite sex. Ellen is "poor little Ellen in her ignorance and simplicity," "my most imprudent little wife," "poor dear good innocent little Ellen," or his "noble little girl." Even her tasks are dwarfed; we see her "busy with her little household arrangements." The fact that her future cousin-in-law, Eleanor, was also of inconsiderable stature was surely an added guarantee of Charley's happiness.

Our first hint that George may have overstated the degree of his cousin's good fortune comes with the wedding itself. Even littleness, apparently, was no proof against nerves.

> The ceremony was badly performed by Dewey. Both parties a good deal agitated — a parlour is far more trying to the nerves than a church. Eleanor saved herself from tears and hysterics and so forth only by a strong and visible effort, for she was evi-

dently in great nervousness and excitement and left the room immediately after the ceremony. I was surprised that Charley felt it so strongly, for I well remember how nonchalant I felt when undergoing the same process, and I was much more likely to have been embarrassed than he. But he was infected, I suppose, by the tremors of his pretty little bride and sympathized in the struggle she was making to control herself.

George, until events later to be recorded, is tactful even in the privacy of his diary about any growth of temperament in Charley's wife. Loyal to Charley, he was presumably working under a presumption in her favor. It is long after the wedding before we discover that all his efforts to promote an intimacy between Eleanor and his own innocent little Ellie have failed from the start. Nor do we have any indication, in these first few years, that Eleanor is subjecting her husband to stormy scenes of willfulness. We see instead the Charley Strongs taking their place with apparent decorum in the social world and attending the Academy of Music with their devoted cousins. In 1851 their only child, Kate, "Miss Puss," was born. The law practice increased, and Charley was duly taken into partnership. Yet there are hints, if carefully watched for, that all is not as it might be in Charley's home. A chapter from George William Curtis' *Nile Notes of a Howadji* has a highly upsetting effect on Eleanor during her pregnancy. While George himself admits that some passages were characterized by "a kind of euphuistic obscenity or puppy-lewdness," Eleanor's reaction of falling into a state of indignant excitement "which might have injured her" seems excessive. Nor is it possible to ascribe this entirely to a moral delicacy that might have justified such immoderation, for in 1855 we find George concerned about Eleanor's unbounded enthusiasm for Rachel, that "Jewish sorceress" whose moral repute was such that she had only been asked once "to meet ladies." Yet we learn that Eleanor "goes every night and experiences fevers and nervous flustrations, with ebullient and explosive hysterical tendencies"! It is hardly a consoling augury.

Eleanor Strong, however, was not to be condemned forever to vicarious excitement. In 1856, the year following that of Rachel's visit, a young journalist and ex-Unitarian minister who also composed hymns and was the author of a travel book of perfervid descriptions, *Gan-Eden, or Pictures of Cuba*, arrived in New York to write for the *New York Times*. William Henry Hurlbert (he had changed it from Hurlbut) is described in the *Dictionary of American Biography* as a "brilliant but erratic genius." He graduated from Harvard Divinity School in 1849, but returned to the university in 1852 for a year of law only to abandon this in turn for his final choice of journalism. Certainly his style was more appropriate to the pages of Putnam's Magazine than to the pulpit or bar. The "L'Envoi" to "Gan-Eden" has the following apostrophe to Cuba:

> *Fair Odalisque upon the purple lying,*
> *Luxurious daughter of the south, farewell!*
> *Upon my ear the palm tree's passionate sighing.*
> *Fades, with the summer sea's voluptuous swell.*

One can imagine that Eleanor Strong, having graduated from a distaste for George William Curtis to a taste for Rachel, might have sighed with the watchers of the north in reading: "I have already spoken of the exceeding beauty of the Cuban nights, and of the golden moon, which pours over the tropical landscape a flood of luxurious splendor, quite unimaginable by those who have but watched her climb the northern skies with a wan face, and with sad steps."

Hurlbert's social success in New York was immediate. He was a facile talker and handsome in a dark mustachioed fashion, and he condescended to the metropolis in a way that nineteenth century New York ladies found agreeable. In his play, *Americans in Paris, or A Game of Dominoes*, he describes their city as "that domestic paradise" and "that Puritanic capital." It is not surprising that George Strong despised him from the very start. His entry for December 6, 1856 reads:

> Hurlbut called here last night to "consult me" about certain matters connected with "the permanent organization of the Republican Party." A

very transparent device, my opinion on any such subject being dear at twopence, and there being no man, woman, or child in the community who thinks it worth more. Mr. Hurlbut simply wants the entrée of this house, which he shan't have till I know more about him. He's very "thick" with sundry of my friends and the place would be convenient. He has a vast social reputation just now, is considered very brilliant and fascinating, is an eminent litterateur in a small way, with political aspirings, has written some respectable little magazine articles for *Putnam* and a readable paper on American Politics in the last *Edinburgh*, and wishes to be considered intimate with the London *Times*. I suspect him of being an unprincipled adventurer, but perhaps I'm wrong.

But, alas, he was not. Only seven months later the diarist plunges us into the center of scandal. It was midsummer of 1857, and George's Ellie had taken the children to Brattleboro while George remained in town to spell Charley at the office. The latter was vacationing with Eleanor in Newport where the "Abbé" Hurlbert, as George sarcastically calls him, was a frequent visitor:

July 31.—Before I was up Charley came to my room just from the Newport boat, the wretched bearer of a lamentable and disgraceful story. Monday afternoon looking for something in his wife's room, he chanced to pick up a letter, and noticed that it was addressed to her in a female hand (Miss E.G.'s to wit) and that the rest of it was in the calligraphy of that treacherous scoundrel, his and her particular friend, the versatile and accomplished Hurlbert. Its recipient had endorsed it on the date of its receipt (that morning) and Charley had himself handed it to her and been told it was from the lady who had written its address and that a book that came with it was one she had promised to send. He read it, and I've read the shameful production. Such a letter as a foolish man would write to his mistress in the first week of concubinage, a letter from which standing alone, anyone would necessarily infer that she who received it had fallen. She came in, admitted that it expressed her actual relations with Hurlbert, denied actual infidelity (which denial I fully credit) and then Charley went to her uncle's cottage (Daniel Butler Fearing) to say that there must be instant and final separation. She was taken by them to their house, and after much discussion with them Charley left for New York.

Hurlbert has been dining with Charley once a week, receiving all manner of hospitality and kindness from him and shewing him studious attention, for near a twelvemonth, and meanwhile has been teaching his wife to lie, and bringing her within a step of adultery. There is more venom in the subtle scoundrel's fluent plausibilities than I gave him credit for. I have always believed that with all her terrible faults, and her entire want of love for her husband, he could trust her anywhere without fear, relying on her constitutional inherent truthfulness of speech and a coldness of temperament. These two safeguards, the sole buttresses of her husband's honor and her own, has this ungrateful disloyal unprincipled adventurer and sophist been able to undermine.

Miss E.G. has not been identified, nor have her friends and co-admirers of Hurlbert, Mrs. P.L. and Mrs. J., soon to appear in the diary. George will have plenty of things to say about this misguided trio, two of whom were apparently related to Eleanor. The time had come for a gathering of the clans, and the ensuing entries show how formidable an opposition could be coalesced in the New York of that day to face an adventurer like Hurlbert. Henry Fearing was the son of Daniel B. Fearing and Eleanor's first cousin. Bob Le Roy, though an alcoholic who eventually died of his failing, was an intimate of all the Strongs. Charles Kuhn had been a sponsor of Hurlbert's, but quickly saw the error of his ways. John Whelten Ehninger and Daniel Messenger were loyal friends of Charley's.

Charley didn't go down town. Wanted me to go to Newport with him. I agreed to do so and spent the morning in much fuss and tribulation — terrible hot day it was — and left on the *Metropolis* at five. Sultry and rueful voyage, a leaden thundercloud dogged us up the

Sound, and soon after we passed Oldfield Light, came down in roaring rain. Got a nap at the Bellevue House and found that Mrs. Charley had been brought back thither by her uncle and was in charge of her cousin Mrs. Allen (who was Miss Mary Watson, most kindly gentle and womanly person she seems). After breakfast drove to Fearing's cottage, leaving Charley at hotel. Took a letter to Fearing and for three hours had it out with him and his sharp Yankee Mrs. Fearing, both protesting and entreating and insisting that separation *must not be*, for the wife's sake. Finally it was settled that Charley should be asked to reconsider. I came off, and concluded to bring him away that evening, for the atmosphere of the place was plainly unwholesome for him. Wrote to Fearing to say so and that Charley for the present adhered to his first decision, but would take time for reflection before acting on it. Walked to the beach; after dinner drove with Charley and Bob Le Roy to *Bateman's* and came off with them both (Ed: returned to New York). Spent most of the night in discussion with Bob, who has some knowledge of the outline of the case, and is rather cynical about it.

Yesterday a day of violent rain. Wrote to Fearing to say that before any action there ought to be some manifesto or statement by the lady of her views of the past, her intentions for the future, her feelings toward her husband. As yet he has had not even a message from her. Indeed she has been confined to her bed, prostrated and hysterical, and he did not see her while at Newport Wednesday. Charles Kuhn taken into confidence, for his own sake.

Today the only new fact is the statement that Hurlbert went to Newport yesterday, which I instantly telegraphed.

I have no doubt there will be an accommodation of this trouble, but it ought to be after a period of suspense and distress that the guilty party will remember, if it ought to be at all. Charley is anxious to shoot the whelp who has done this mischief and treason, but I guess I can prevent a collision, even if the matter become public, so that a row would not be inadmissable as compromising the lady. Poor foolish illregulated girl, muddled with French novels and by a life of idleness (for her husband took every household duty off her hands long ago). I'm indignant with her half the time, or so bitterly sorry for her the other half.

August 1. Saturday evening. Events progress, and my Scandalous Chronicle flourishes. First came Daniel Fearing with a report that Hurlbert was at Newport yesterday and wanted to see the lady — didn't of course — then Hurlbert came to Fearing's house taking a position in their brief interview the reverse of contrite or humble but what precisely Fearing could not make out intelligibly to me. He cleared out at half past two for New York. Fearing reports Mrs. Charley still in bed and much prostrated, very penitent and prepared to make every pledge for the future. Brought a brief note to her husband, dry and cold, but better than I expected. It must be remembered that she's really ill and very weak and that she never has any facility on paper. It may do for a beginning.

Next came a letter of eight pages from the Abbé Hurlbert to *me*, as Charley's friend, inviting an interview and setting forth his views. Either he is insane, or he feels himself in a horribly false position and wants to cover his retreat by bullying. I replied by a dry note, refusing to recognize his *right to be a party to any settlement between Charley and his wife* (!!! incredible as it seems, that is the ground he takes and unless that be acceded to, he has the inconceivable baseness to threaten to blow the whole affair) and telling him I'd be home at eight tonight, if he wanted to say anything that would enable me to be of service to the lady or the gentleman. I don't believe he'll come. Nothing can exceed the audacious assumptions of right to act for Mrs. Charley, to dictate terms as to what licence her husband is to allow her in case of reconciliation, etc. etc., of which his letter is full. Should he come this evening we shall have a precious time.

Later. He didn't come at all. Went with Charley to John Whetten Ehninger's without finding him and waited for him some time in vain. Charley wants to make him a confidant, in view of ulterior measures, a demand for surrender of the letters, and physical force if Hurlbert decline. Think of his holding them, refusing to deliver them to Miss E.G. on the written request of their penitent authoress, and threatening to publish them if his demands be not complied with! And of his talking about "Christian morals and public order" being promoted by his exaggerated and extravagant baseness!

August 2. Sunday night. That man Hurlbert has been twice in this house today. Do not its walls need ceremonial purification? The glass from which some water was given this dog when he was (unless he were shamming) overpowered by agitation, I have smashed. No guest of mine shall run the risk of catching his foul disease. Things look bad and black; the two Fearings and Jack Ehninger have just gone. Charley, poor fellow, has gone to bed; he spends tonight here.

To church this morning (Trinity Chapel). Saw Rev. Hobart, whose advice Charley wanted as to what would be right and what wrong. It was still an open question this morning whether Charley ought to take her back and plain that he ought at least to hold off long enough to give her a stern lesson. Went to 34th St. with Hobart, and put him in possession of all material facts. Ehninger, Henry Fearing and Charley dined here, and after dinner Ehninger and Fearing went off to see Hurlbert. *He* (Ed: Hurlbert) called a few minutes after to state that I was mistaken in my suggestion of yesterday as to the lady's views and wishes; he had received a letter "from Newport yesterday" confirming his opinion on that subject. Farthermore, he was going thither this week. He was very urbane, and I equally so, but put of course the utmost possible formality and repulsion into my manner. Interview was very short. Went as fast as possible after our two friends; found them by great good fortune. Henry Fearing was taken all aback by this new and most alarming phase. He was for very prompt and conclusive action, and I had hard work to get him to temporize a little. They went after him (Ed: Hurlbert) again, having spent a couple of hours here in debate, at the hour he told me he would be at his rooms, but didn't find him, returned chafing and disappointed. Charley went off to see Hobart, and then this traitor came once more and was received in the library Fearing being speaker, we two merely auditors, a condition Fearing insisted on. The man's decision, promptitude and infernal composure and audacity were appalling. He refused to say anything about the letter from Newport unless with Fearing alone. Jack and I withdrew to the dining room. Daniel Fearing came, and after a time his son came down in an agony of rage and sorrow.

It was too true. The poor weak girl had written Friday (the very day she wrote her husband) a lamentable letter to Mrs. P.L. — "Her relatives were giving her no peace" — "He ought to go to Europe" — "We shall meet again soon" — "Should her husband refuse to receive her, her only hope is in *him*."

The woman (Ed: Mrs. P.L.) had given Hurlbert that letter! Are the ladies of New York to turn procuresses?

Has Hurlbert promised that unprincipled daughter of a swindling financier a commission on the fortune of the victim she is helping him to run down?

At first it seemed that all was lost — perhaps it is — but we've rallied a little.

Hurlbert went out of the house soon after, by the door and not through the window, a shameful fact; he was not insulted, but he did hear, thank Heaven, some pretty plain truths conveyed in conventional circumlocution. He seeks a quarrel and an exposure and thinks he can force it by going to Newport. There he supposes reconciliation impossible and that the lady will seek his protection. With her fortune they could live abroad, at least till he was tired of her, and he can always support himself by his wits and his pen. Loss of position here would be a matter of indifference to a mere nomadic adventurer. That is his game, and he's playing it boldly and well, utterly unscrupulous now as to the means he uses. By the blessing of Heaven he shall be defeated, and the lady shall return to her duty.

But alas for her husband — what a home will his be — and how many dreary years he must pass before there can be a germ of returning affection, even if all go smoothly and well, as it hardly can even if this persevering intriguer abandon the siege. And it is yet uncertain whether this *coup de main* will be repulsed, uncertain how the lady will decide.

August 3. Monday night. Another letter to me from

Hurlbert this morning, opening a new abyss of infamy. It contains a quotation from that lady's (Ed: Eleanor's) Newport letter (how her uncle and aunt "*do not know all*" or they wouldn't urge her to go back) which is meant to convey, doubtless, the worst insinuation against her. And of its falsehood no one has any doubt. *She* means that they are ignorant of some fancied wrong or injury by her husband. He means to suggest to her husband that she has *fallen* and thus raise a new barrier to reconciliation, *the caitiff*.

I'm very anxious and unhappy tonight. If this man seek to force his way to the lady's presence he will be *shot down*. And I fear a duel; my only hope is in the strong suspicion he's a coward.

August 4. Tuesday night. Very warm day, ending in a muggy cloudy evening, with rain falling steadily and straight down through the stagnant air. Have been very busy and much worried closing up one or two real estate transactions that I never heard of till the papers were handed me to be delivered or exchanged.

Three or four despatches this morning from Henry Fearing, the last dated 1.15 P.M. The lady is said to have "promised everything" of her own free will. She's at Fearing's cottage.

Hurlbert did not leave town and is not going to Newport. Dan Messenger has had a long talk with him and was to have had another this afternoon. Messenger assumed the position of friend to the lady, exclusively acting in the interests of no other person. By his account he manipulated this unclean and dangerous beast to some good purpose and brought him to pledge himself to stay in town, to admit that an explosion ought to be averted, not encouraged, and that he must "efface himself" and make no claim "to be a party" to any settlement. He is or pretends to be in a high strung intense excitement and sensitiveness, avows a state of Idolatry, highfalutin' reverence (!) and the like. She's his sole inspiration, the only thing he lives for, source of every virtuous and exalted impulse etcetera, a sort of Platonico-erotico Delirium Tremens.

God help poor Charley through these troublesome times and through the weary years that will follow, when the excitement of the crisis is over and he feels only the depression of his dismal home and the dead weight of the unloving wife to whom he's chained. For they will come together again, I think, beyond doubt. They ought to, if only that this beast may not triumph.

August 5. Wednesday night. Thank God, I believe this poor wrongheaded girl is safe, not from guilt only but from scandal. Henry Fearing came here early this morning and I'd a letter from her husband beside. They agree that her course has been better than they'd hoped: entire penitence, deep mortification, something like an expression of *wifely* feeling, and infinite disgust at the baseness of her fluent friend with the moustache. She promises everything and says she'd try to keep her promises, but knows she may fail. So far well. But all impressions on her are evanescent; any new excitement wipes them out. Probably she'll forget this particular vagabond within two weeks, but hopes founded on her faculty of self denial, self control, common sense and steadiness of purpose cannot be sanguine. She gave Henry Fearing a letter authorizing him to demand of that ornament to society (Ed: Hurlbert) her late correspondence, all letters in his possession; this Fearing gave to Messenger, and Messenger took it to the Abbé's. The Abbé has been sustaining his valuable existence for some days past (Ed: several words erased) and cigars exclusively. His nerves are naturally shaky. He spent an hour stamping about the room, in a semi-maudlin semi-hysterical state, tearing his hair, gnashing his teeth, rolling his fine eyes and knocking his intellectual nob against the wall, like an exasperated bluebottle fly, and finally fell down in a species of caniption fit and foamed at the mouth, and lay for some time in rigors and coma. Messenger stood still and called in no help, the man being in a phrenetic condition and liable to make indiscreet disclosures if he came to. Messenger thought it best to permit the Destinies to have their own way, and let the man die "dacently" without disgracing himself any more. But he picked himself up at last and the upshot was an agonized consent to surrender the letters tomorrow.

It's really pitiful to think that the little brimstone (Ed: Eleanor) who has caused all this mess and given this featherbrained poetaster these spasms and paroxysms, don't in truth care two pence for him, has encouraged his devotion, because it gratified her vanity and gave her a new excitement, and wouldn't sacrifice one atom of social status, or risk losing an invitation to one "nice party" for the sake of all the accomplished Hurlberts between South Carolina and Cape Cod.

August 6. Thursday. Telegraph informs me that affairs are in so satisfactory a condition at Newport that my unhappy friend (Ed: Charley) there wants to get back to Wall Street.

Among the absurdest scenes ever acted on the surface of this planet, by the by, must have been his (Ed: Hurlbert's) last interview with that goodnatured phlegmatic lump of sound practical common sense, Daniel Messenger. An able editor, accomplished scholar and most fascinating member of polite society going about on all fours, raving and roaring, stopping now and then to *bite* another man's fat legs, tenderly apostrophizing [him] sometimes as "his own dearest Eleanor," sometimes adjuring him (as Mrs. J.) to go to his said dearest and tell her to come and put herself under his protection, and sometimes whispering to him (as his dearest's husband) chokily and grimly that he intended to "cut his heart out" at the first convenient opportunity, is a spectacle seldom vouchsafed to admirers of the ridiculous. It's very refreshing besides to find something to laugh at in the performance of so desperately efficient an agent of mischief.

August 17. Monday evening. Letters from Charley during my absence. He's unhappy and despondent about the future, no wonder. I can see that the impression made by even this most narrow escape, on the person whose caprices and fancies are to determine so much of his future, is half-obliterated already. What has he ever done that this calamity should visit him? What have I ever done, that my lot should be so different?

One of the silly sentimental women who have been officiating as bawds in this transaction, without sense enough to be aware of their function, has written a delicious letter of congratulation to the lady (Ed: Eleanor) on the amicable adjustment of her troubles, full of eulogy on her husband's nobleness and generosity, just what she would have expected of one whom she has always upheld as among the most admirable of men!! She must be among the shallowest and most sneaking of women.

August 20. Thursday. Wonderful that the Hurlbert transaction has been kept so close, for at least thirty people know of it. Some leakage is absolutely inevitable.

Charley came to town Tuesday reporting everything at Newport *couleur de rose*, contrition and good resolutions, and the horizon far clearer and the prospect of fair weather more hopeful than any time for the last five years. But he's not sanguine about the future and has no right to be so.

The position of these three women (Mrs. J., Mrs. P.L., Miss E.G.) has changed. They are now furious with our poor little friend because she didn't run away from her husband after all. "She is not the woman they took her to be, and they're satisfied now that she's incapable of true affection." Really it's like the wrath of one of the Mercer Street aristocracy when a new recruit has failed to keep an appointment and offended a customer.

I'm horribly tired of the whole botheration and trust it will soon be over.

August 21. Friday night. Letter from great Hurlbert this morning, amounting to very little, and winding up with a well turned expression of pleasure that the imbroglio is settled to everybody's satisfaction. He has evidently made up his mind that it's best for him to let it be finished up and forgotten with all convenient speed. All I hear of him leads me to believe that his moral vision is organically defective, like the retina in color blindness. His miserable habit of taking counsel of women in all his scrapes, instead of advising with men, makes the consequences of this infirmity worse. He has beyond question a strange uncanny snakey power of fascinating silly females, and winning them to reverent unquestioning faith in his infallibility and goodness. They endorse his suggestions and strengthen his convictions. No stronger proof of his power over them can be found than this case presents. Not to speak of his principal victim, or of two of the three ladies whom he puts forward as his allies and advisers, the third in that blessed Pas de seduction (Miss G. to wit) has always passed for a sensible good hearted old maid, pious after the Unitarian fashion, abundant in good works, *virtuous* at least, yet she is perfectly ignorant that she has been the cat'spaw of a scoundrel and sympathizes deeply with him in his heroic sorrow that he as principal and she as doorkeeper failed to corrupt her kinswoman and dearest friend.

Charley has been here this evening and I've administered to him a strong dose of counsel. He had proposed that Miss G. above referred to be not absolutely cut off from his acquaintance. I tell him that decency and prudence and the inherent fitness of things require that she never darken his doors again.

There remained only the dry matters of dropping all intercourse with Mrs. J., Mrs. P.L. and Miss E.G. and of liquidating the remnants of Hurlbert's social reputation. Charley, however, to his cousin's dismay, continued to show an "inexcusable and almost criminal" weakness about cutting his wife off from Miss G.'s society, and the friends had to be reassembled to bolster his faltering will. A letter was opportunely produced in which the abandoned Miss G., clearly devoid of all instincts on which rested "the whole nature of pure women," actually purported to justify Hurlbert's conduct! George, after reading the letter, had to go out in the bright moonlight and sea breeze to walk it off. Yet even then Charley begged that his wife be allowed to retain a formal acquaintance! Daniel Messenger, who was evidently the peacemaker of the group, brought up the suggestion that Miss G. might have been under a misapprehension as to Eleanor's relationship with Hurlbert, that she might have innocently supposed it to be only the exchange of "literary and aesthetic raptures." It was agreed that Miss G. be given one more chance and confronted with the famous letter that had precipitated the whole crisis. If after reading *that*, she did not forever repudiate Hurlbert, they would know how to deal with her. George, still skeptical, nonetheless agreed to act as their ambassador.

I thought that it would do no manner of good, but it was settled I should call on her, and she honored me with an invitation to do so this evening. I was reluctant to shew her this letter, which compromises so deeply the person to whom it was sent and concluded to ask two preliminary questions before shewing it. The questions were: 1. Did you suppose the relations of these parties to be amatory or merely those of warm friendship? 2. If you see evidence that they were of the former type, will you repudiate your friend Hurlbert? I did not get beyond No. 1. The harridan said with the utmost frankness and simplicity that she knew their correspondence was "ardent and passionate." Whereupon I expressed my regret at having trespassed on her time and walked away as fast as possible. The Destinies clearly meant her to keep a genteel establishment in Mercer Street.

The fatal letter which I read this evening for the first

time since the day the explosion was announced to me is even worse than my recollections of it. Any woman who receives such a letter, and puts it quietly away, has little left to lose; the inevitable act of adultery is mere matter of form, and in the case of any other woman than this I should infer that her criminality had been formally consummated already. Then comes her damning duplicity in writing to her two *bawds* in New York to tell Hurlbert *she* "did not doubt him or want her letters returned, it was her Uncle and her Aunt who insisted on their surrender," on the very day she was professing herself penitent and asking her husband's forgiveness. She's past hope I fear, only not quite as bad as this Miss E.G. They must be vagarics of nature, abnormal departures from the law of their sex. It cannot be that our women are becoming unwomanly disloyal and impure.

After this even Charley collapsed and meekly agreed to write Miss G. a sixteen page letter drafted by George informing her that a "total non-intercourse" would be established between the two households and comparing her propositions "in the plainest terms polite language would allow with the commonly received notions about adultery and pimping." Before Charley's letter had even been sent, however, the incurable Miss G. threw her last shred of principle to the winds and defiantly wrote Eleanor to urge her to leave her false life and go back to her true love. No walk in the seabreeze could help

George to get over this one. In a wholesome society, he expostulates, such a woman would be "pilloried in the Park or flogged at the cart's tail." If his diary is Dickensian in its rapturous passages, it can suggest *Hamlet* in its invective:

> No harridan of Church Street ever talked braver pathos to a timid recruit. The woman must be diseased in mind; if she be sane, her vicious effrontery is the most appalling crime that has occurred in the decent strata of society within my time. For she has no passion to palliate her profligacy; she is past the hotblooded period of life, when sheer *lust* might be gratified in some morbid way by peering through keyholes at a progressive intrigue, and when an impure woman might itch to be an accessory to the impurity of others. She is not even a fool like her colleague Mrs. L., but is rather intelligent, old, out of health, and performs her filthy function in cold blood and with her eyes open. Unless she be a monomaniac on the subject of the great Hurlbert and all his doings she is something not adequately to be expressed in polite language. Enough of her.

The ostracization of Hurlbert himself proceeded with more despatch. There was no trouble here with Charley. In fact George was even concerned that his cousin might go too far. He had to dissuade him from writing formally to one Charles Kingsley to enquire if the latter had really *advised* Hurlbert to be such a scoundrel. With people who had never endorsed Hurlbert's misconduct, however, Charley was more discreet. He gave a hint of Hurlbert's unworthiness, without descending to particulars, to Lewis Jones who, in George's opinion, was one of "the strongest and finest grained of our young men." Jones reacted promptly. When Hurlbert next called at his house on 16th Street, he was not admitted and received word from Mrs. Jones that she was acting on her husband's instructions. The unrebuffable Hurlbert called again and insisted on seeing the master of the house to find out on what stories the latter had acted. Jones replied icily that he chose to exercise the privilege of selecting his own and his wife's acquaintance.

The unfortunate Hurlbert now found himself up against a small but tightly knit New York. When he wrote a "charming episotelette" to Mrs. Sally Hampton, asking when he might call to present his homages, it was returned by her husband with a brief note declining all further intercourse and warning him that any attempt to renew the acquaintance would be regarded as a personal affront. George Strong, finding himself buttonholed by James W. Otis in pursuit of knowledge of Hurlbert, enlightened him with "the driest facts, using no epithets and withholding names." The indefatigable diarist was not averse to taking advantage of prejudices that had nothing to do with the case. When John

Church Hamilton, son of Alexander, asked his opinion of Hurlbert and, receiving it, intimated that the latter would be excluded thenceforth from the "Palazzo Hamilton," George confides to his diary that what really incensed Hamilton was the *Times*' criticism of his biography of his father, with which Hurlbert, in actual fact, had had nothing to do. But severest of all was George's attitude to a Mr. and Mrs. Beals, who had continued to receive Hurlbert in spite of the ban. Providence seems to have come to his aid in dealing with these recalcitrants for in October following the summer events Mr. Beals not only developed a fatal illness, but his business was ruined. His wife, in the greatest distress, begged to see her friend Eleanor, but George, inexorable, had "to advise Charley to be hardhearted and to refuse his wife permission to enter any house frequented by Hurlbert."

Hurlbert decided to leave New York; one cannot believe that he had much alternative. He moved to England where George notes sourly that he was much lionized. He was back in New York the following year but only for a visit, and he steered clear of all Strongs. Unhappily, however, his departure did little to promote the reconciliation of Charley and Eleanor. As George had noted, the trouble was basically in his cousin's wife. The marriage held together through the war, but shortly afterwards, in the spring of 1866, Eleanor and Miss Puss went abroad to live, and Charley sold the house on 22nd Street and moved into bachelor quarters. Yet even in Paris, George ruefully notes two years later, Eleanor's sensibility continued to lure her down strange paths:

> Charley Strong shewed me this morning, rather ruefully, a letter just received from Madame at Paris, announcing her "reconciliation" to the Roman Catholic Church. Just what has long been predicted. The lady is a strange compound of cleverness and foolishness; she is jaded with French novels; she wants a new sensation, and she has been talked over by experts in the art of conversion, French and English priests, flattered and caressed and wound round their fingers. Her letter is well written, however, and she declares she will scrupulously abstain from influencing dear little Pussy. I don't expect she will take much trouble to do so, of her own volition. But her Spiritual Directors will enjoin it on her as a duty, and Pussy will be somehow manoeuvred into Popedom before she knows it. Much as I like the mamma, and fully as I recognize her brightness and her many good points, I cannot help seeing that in this transaction, as in many other grave transactions of her married life, she has behaved like a goose.

Hurlbert left behind him, at least in the Strong circle, a reputation of evil incarnate. The diary does not become more forgiving as the years ensue. In 1864 he is described as a "coprophagous" insect and as late as 1872 as "a gaudily-colored and fetid bug . . . among the basest of mankind." The villain, Densdeth, in the posthumously published novel, *Cecil Dreeme*, by George's friend Theodore Winthrop, who fell at Big Bethel, was supposedly based on Hurlbert. The hero, while waiting to see if the villain will ensnare him, becomes involved in an emotional friendship with a pale young man who, to the reader's relief, turns out in the end to be the heroine disguised in male garb. She, too, is hiding from Densdeth. Why they are all so afraid of Densdeth and how he obtains his hold over them is obscure. He simply radiates wickedness:

> Presently, as I glanced up and down the table, I caught sight of Densdeth's dark, handsome face. He had turned from his companion, and was looking at me. He lifted his black moustache with a slight sneer . . . "What does it mean," thought I, "this man's strange fascination? When his eyes are upon me, I feel something stir in my heart, saying, 'Be Densdeth's! He knows the mystery of life.' I begin to dread him. Will he master my will? What is this potency of his? How has he got this lodgment in my spirit? Is he one of those fabulous personages who only exist while they are preying upon another soul, who are torpid unless they are busy contriving damnation?"

The half-comic note of the villain of melodrama may give us the ultimate clue to poor Hurlbert. He was certainly more ridiculous than sinister. It is hard to imagine wickedness in a man whose art gallery, according to an 1883 auction catalogue, contained such titles as "Halt of Cavaliers," "The First Dancing Lesson," "The Abbess Detected" and "Toilette of the Odalisque." It is easier to see him as vain, flashy, eager to please and appallingly sentimental, with a kind of florid charm and a gift of always putting his foot in things, which might have been forgiven had he not insisted on explaining his good intentions. To the end he explained, and with increasing shrillness. Small wonder that people found him exasperating. He was imprisoned in Richmond during the war as a suspected Union agent, yet, released, he stumped for McClellan on a campaign of peace at any price. He advocated the cause of royalism in France of the eighteen-seventies and fought home rule in Ireland under a Gladstone government. Yet he was always vivid; it is possible even today to read his angry books. And he was successful. From 1876 to 1883 he was editor-in-chief of the New York *World*.

At the age of fifty-seven Hurlbert drastically altered his life. He resigned from the *World*, married (for the first time) a Miss Katherine Parker Tracy, sold his art collection and moved to London. If, however, he was looking for peace and quiet after the stormy years, he was not to find it. For it was in London, the capital of justice, that he encountered the final wrong from a universe that seemed always to have conspired against him.

In 1891 a woman named Gertrude Ellis, describing herself as an actress and living under the name of Gladys Evelyn, sued him for £10,000, alleging that in 1887 he had seduced her under promise of marriage three weeks after their casual meeting as fellow passengers in a London omnibus. She further alleged that Hurlbert had hidden his true identity under the pseudonym of Wilfred Murray and that she had lost track of him until another chance meeting in a London street when she had followed him to his house. At the trial, which stirred up considerable public feeling against Hurlbert, Mrs. Ellis was unable to produce any witness who had seen her with the defendant except one individual who was proved to have been her lover. She did produce, however, a batch of obscene letters allegedly written by Hurlbert which were impounded by the court. Hurlbert won his case, and the verdict was sustained on appeal, but when he attempted to obtain the letters as a basis for criminal proceedings against Mrs. Ellis, he was met with a curt refusal. It was the court's opinion that the plaintiff should not be exposed to prosecution because of a technical inability to prove her case. There was also the fact that the attorney-general wanted the letters as the basis for a possible prosecution of Hurlbert himself. Hurlbert, however, persisted with his demands until Lord Chief Justice Coleridge himself was obliged to explain the position of the court to the House of Lords. He managed to do so in a way that tarnished even further the defendant's good name:

> My Lords, I ought to say that of Mr. Hurlbut personally I know nothing whatever. I never saw him, I never met him, I never read a word of his writing, I am absolutely ignorant of him; whether he is entitled to the description which an illustrious American gave of him, namely that he is a man of fathomless and measureless turpitude, or whether he is a person entitled to the eulogiums which have been passed upon him, and the respect, admiration and intimacy, which have been given to him by persons of very high rank in this country, I neither know nor care.

It is impossible not to speculate on the identity of the "illustrious American." Could he have been one of the thirty to whom the now ancient secret of Newport had been divulged? We know enough of Hurlbert, anyway, to be sure that he would not let this pass. The man who had been so eager to defend his position in 1857 was not one to bow even to the House of Lords in 1893. Old and bitter, he pulled himself together for a final outburst of self-vindication which appeared in the form of a privately printed volume of more than 500 pages entitled *England under Coercion: a Record of Private Rights Outraged and of Public Justice Betrayed by Political Malice for Partisan Ends, set forth as in a letter to the Lord Coleridge, Lord Chief Justice of England*. This remarkable document can be read as the final symptom of a galloping persecution mania, or, theoretically at least, as a statement of the true facts. Reading it, one remembers the long distant scene when the author writhed on the floor before Daniel Messenger. From all its strange ramblings, its curious irrelevancies, its venom and its quaint oratory, the argument emerges that a powerful political conspiracy has been hatched to discredit Hurlbert as the author of a book, published years previously, that was unsympathetic to Irish home rule. Gertrude Ellis and her shabby little suit have become a snare set by the highest officers of the British crown for an American who dared to speak his mind!

> I leave you here arraigned, my Lord [he concludes], as the prime cause and author of such a series of outrages and wrongs perpetrated under the prostituted forms of English law upon me . . . Does the great commission which you hold put you beyond the reach of justice and of the laws and leave you free without responsibility to perpetrate and to promote such outrages and such wrongs under the coercion of political schemes and of partisan passion? Do the laws of England leave absolutely without remedy or redress every British subject and every foreign resident within the realm of England who may suffer at your hands and through you such outrages and wrongs?

The year that his defense was published was the last year of Hurlbert's life. He died in Italy with an English warrant still out against him for perjury in connection with the trial. It seems quite possible that in the end he had run into a real injustice. Many of his friends believed so. But we can doubt if George Strong would ever have been convinced that his "gaudily colored" bug was not the guilty party of Evelyn *v.* Hurlbert. We are denied his opinion, however, for the diarist had died long before, in 1875. His cousin, Charley, respected and admired, an eminent leader of the bar, survived his old rival, dying in his house at 16 Fifth Avenue in 1897. Eleanor Strong, despite a diagnosis of "incurable tumors" as early as 1870, lived into this century. The New York Social Register records her death in Florence in 1903.

A Reader's Guide to the Fiction of Henry James

IN APPROACHING the great prolific novelists of the last century, it is usually safe for the uninitiated reader to start at the top, with *Vanity Fair* for Thackeray or *David Copperfield* for Dickens. But nobody should try to begin Henry James with *The Golden Bowl.* And if the beginner should happen to start with *The Awkward Age* and to follow it with *The Sacred Fount,* he might well be conditioned for life to finding nothing but snobbishness and triviality in any of the other works. It is better to face at the outset that there will always be a certain number of people to agree with Theodore Roosevelt's dictum that James's "polished, pointless, uninteresting stories about the upper social classes of England make one blush to think that he was once an American." It is not, however, necessary to turn, instead, as Roosevelt did, to the "fresh, healthy, out-of-doors life" of

Kipling. One can learn, with a little application, to isolate the dross in James, and after that *The Jungle Book* is no substitute. Once the reader has been acclimatized to the different Jamesian styles, once he has felt the intensity of that devotion to his aesthetic ideal, he can be safely exposed even to such dreary minor pieces as *Glasses* or *Fordham Castle.* Who knows? He may even like them. For by that time he will be a Jacobite, and the true Jacobite can delight in any prose of the master.

James himself was once consulted on the order in which he should be read. In 1913 he made two reading lists for Stark Young, "the delightful young man from Texas." But he omitted the short stories (the "little tarts" could wait until after the "beef and potatoes"), and he insisted (contrary to the advice of many of his critics) on being read in the revised edition. Each of his suggested reading lists contains only five titles, the first: *Roderick Hudson*, *The Portrait of a Lady*, *The Princess Casamassima*, *The Wings of the Dove*, *The Golden Bowl*, and the second: *The American*, *The Tragic Muse*, *The Wings of the Dove*, *The Ambassadors*, *The Golden Bowl.* Both lists have in common with this piece the goal of bringing the new reader as rapidly as possible to what E. M. Forster calls the "valuable and exquisite sensations" of the final novels. But it seems to me that the recommended steps are too short and that *Roderick Hudson* is an actual stumbling block. That James was not the best judge of his own earlier work is shown by his omission of *Washington Square* and *The Bostonians* from the revised edition. My purpose is to present a somewhat more comprehensive list for the beginner, and with this in mind I have divided James's writing life into five periods: beginnings, 1866–1880; the "Balzac" period, 1880–1890; experiments with the theatre, 1890–1895; the "bad" period, 1895–1901, and the final greatness, 1901–1911.

First (1866–1880). This initial period opens with a great clump of short stories reminiscent in style and treatment of Hawthorne. They are well organized and smoothly written, but they incline at once to the prolix and melodramatic. There is little in them to distinguish James from other young American writers of the period, full of Europe after a first grand tour. The reader, like one of the characters, may feel himself an innocent American, visiting a *pension* on his first trip abroad and speculating on the history of the old lady in black who never speaks to anybody, or of the mysterious professor, or of the guileless ingenue, or of her formidable mother who may have designs on a stout young fellow like himself. For the point of view from which these tales are told is not that of the subtle, shadowy, dedicated, keyhole listener of later periods (*The Sacred Fount*), but of the stalwart Harvard man with a bit more than a gentleman's interest in old churches and pictures — yet very much the gentleman for all that — who likes his pipe and his wine and his club and who occasionally steps out of the role of narrator to direct the action himself. "I drew her arm into mine, and before the envious eyes that watched us from gilded casements we passed through the gallery and left the palace." The James of the second period begins to emerge in *The American* and *The Europeans* and comes out altogether in that exquisite little novel, *Washington Square*, where in the ordered stillness of a mid-Victorian New York a girl's happiness is snuffed out by a father who has the vice of being always right.

Second (1880–1890). This I have called the "Balzac" period. James may have felt in this decade that he had settled on the kind of novel that he would write for the rest of his life: the three-volume Balzacian compendium of diverse characters plotted around a contemporary social problem. To many readers this is his finest period. Surely it is hard to pick and choose among such novels as *The Portrait of a Lady* (the conflict between Americans soiled and Americans unsoiled by a dark, beautiful, ancient Europe); *The Bostonians* (the cause of women's suffrage as an arena for sex antagonism); *The Princess Casamassima* (the danger that world revolution may destroy more than it brings), and *The Tragic Muse* (the question of art as a substitute for a political career). The style of these novels is of a dazzling virtuosity; there are passages in *The Portrait of a Lady* and *The Bostonians* as beautiful as any prose James ever wrote. Had he died in his middle forties instead of seventies, he would still be regarded as a master of American fiction. It must, also, have been a period of happiness; I am sure he had a deep satisfaction in feeling his feet on sure ground and seeing ahead the long straight road of a dozen or more novels dealing with the rich themes of the impact of art and socialism and Americans on an established Victorian social order. There is an exuberance in the very speed with which the novels were written; *The Bostonians* and *The Princess Casamassima* appeared in the same year. Yet none of them attained the success of *Daisy Miller*, and James cared about success. How could he not have? He lived in a society which considered it all-important, and he lacked the substitutes of a profession, a family or a fortune. The inner buoyancy of knowing that he had written such a book as *Portrait of a Lady* was not enough. He turned, like so many others then and now, to the theatre, to try to master its trick and achieve the fame that he craved. Perhaps had he been less sure that it was a trick, he would have succeeded better.

Third (1890–1895). This is the period of dramatic experiment, ending with the famous booing of the author at the opening of *Guy Domville*. James to his dying day insisted that he owed a great debt to the theatre, that out of the wreck of his experiments he saved a sense of the dramatic that was to be invaluable in the construction of the later novels. Knowing how desperately authors hate to think of any writing efforts as wasted, I allow myself to doubt this. The dramatic in James's plays (such as it is) strikes me as having very little to do with the dramatic in the later novels. The only thing remarkable to me about James's plays is that any were produced at all. They read like thin, wordy parodies of his poorest fiction and are pervaded with a repellent heartlessness. The bad writing of a professional is like that of an amateur. Bits and pieces of his personality keep showing like slips under a skirt. One of the reasons we are so apt to feel that we could be friends with great authors is that their expert prose covers the smaller side of their natures. James's plays should be concealed at all cost from the would-be Jacobite. He wrote no novels in this period, but he kept his fictional hand at work with a series of perfect short stories, including "The Death of the Lion" and "Greville Fane," written in a clear, finished style that lacks the verbosity of his first period and the involutions of his last. Perhaps these stories also lack some of the warmth and color of the prose of his *Portrait of a Lady* period; there is a certain thinness of material and a growing preoccupation with the fantastic and supernatural. But if there are less high points in this period, there are no low ones. The beginner may roam at will from "The Lesson of the Master" to "The Altar of the Dead."

Fourth (1895–1901). This is what I call the "bad" period, to be avoided almost entirely until the reader is a converted Jacobite. Biographically it is interesting, for it reveals a James struggling to pull out of the disappointment of his failure as a dramatist and popular novelist and to achieve his own unique medium. But such a struggle was bound to be saturated with the bitterness that had caused it, and some of this bitterness creeps into his work, giving it a peculiar shrillness, even, at times, a silliness. There is a triviality in the themes that no amount of good writing can succeed in making important. Peeping behind the curtain of art at the author's small resentments, we glimpse the diner-out who is obsessed with the decline of manners in London high life, the aesthete who prefers houses and ornaments to people, the prude who is shocked by sex. Of course, all of these attitudes can be found in the earlier and in the later work: Hyacinth Robinson in *The Princess Casamassima* (1886) gives up his plans for world revolution because it might muddy the translucent waters of the aristocratic way of life, the contemplation of which must be the eternal solace of the poor, and *A Round of Visits* (1910) transfers the author's high-pitched anger at London hostesses to those of New York. But it is in this "bad" period that these attitudes seem most, as James himself would put it, to "bristle." It is the period of the damp, crushed spinster heroines, of Fleda Vetch and the telegraph girl of *In the Cage*, who live to observe and observe to live, who can never quite handle the overwhelming, suffocating vulgarity that surrounds them. Like Maisie, they know everything, but their comfort is in renunciation, a renunciation that smacks of a disdain to participate.

Too many Jacobites have tried to explain away the

silliness of this period by reading other things into it. I think it is better to face it directly like the audiences of *The High Bid* (James's dramatization of *Covering End*) who burst into applause, to the dismay of the author, when Captain Yule cried out: "I see something else in the world than the beauty of old show-houses and the glory of old show-families. There are thousands of people in England who can show no houses *at all*, and I don't feel it utterly shameful to share their poor fate!"

The best writing of this period is in *The Spoils of Poynton* which prefigures James's ultimate style, but the masterpiece is "The Turn of the Screw." Perhaps one of the reasons for its success is that James never tells us explicitly of what the "evil" consists. If it is simply that Quilt and Miss Jessel have an affair which has not been concealed from the children, I feel that the author has taken advantage, however skillfully, of my propensity to panic.

Fifth (1902–1911). Quite suddenly we emerge from the timber into the high, golden light of the final period and meet in dazzling succession the three last novels, *The Wings of the Dove*, *The Ambassadors* and *The Golden Bowl*. These have created for James the special niche in the history of literature that was the objective of a lifetime of devoted work. Gone now is the shrill anger at bad manners and sexual irregularity. A benign wisdom pervades the atmosphere. The evil in

The Wings of the Dove is not in the affair between Kate Croy and Merton Densher; it is in their concealment of it from an ailing girl whose money they want. When Densher pounds the streets of a storm-swept Venice while Milly Theale faces a lonely death in her palazzo, we know, as nowhere in the earlier James, the agony of remorse. And in *The Ambassadors* when Strether at last discovers what everyone else has always known, that Chad Newsome is living with Madame de Vionnet, that he is enjoying the common-or-garden love affair with the older married woman that is the conventional oat-sowing of the rich young American before his return to the family business, there is no implication that Chad is "evil." It has simply been Strether's naïveté that has made him see another relationship in the affair. But this very naïveté, stripped of James's earlier bitterness and radiant with a new perception, is what lifts Strether above Chad and his mistress. As E. M. Forster puts it: "The Paris they revealed to him — he could reveal it to them now, if they had eyes to see, for it is something finer than they could ever notice for themselves, and his imagination has more spiritual value than their youth."

The themes of the three great novels are worthy of the prose which develops them. There is nothing trivial in Kate Croy's conspiracy to have her lover inherit Milly's money, or in Maggie Verver's efforts to save her own and her father's marriages. But the greatest theme of all is that of *The Ambassadors:* the self-reeducation of an elderly man who is not afraid to make the count of all that he has missed in life. There is none of the contrived aspect of some of James's fictional *données*, yet the plot is the most neatly balanced of all the novels. W. D. Howells' exhortation to the young man in Whistler's garden to live life to the fullest and not to waste his youth was the seed from which the masterpiece sprang. The subject was right; the style was ready, and *The Ambassadors* was written with a confident speed. To me it is the perfect novel.

The remaining stories, except for "The Jolly Corner," represent a falling off to be expected in old age. The subject matter is trivial again, the style even more elaborate. One senses the aging master, sure now of a small but devoted following who will wait indefinitely for the *mot juste;* we can almost hear the prefatory cough, the chuckle as it is finally produced and dangled before their gleaming eyes. But we must not expect the moon. The master had already given us his best.

Like James himself I would submit two lists to the "delightful young man from Texas" of today. My first I believe to be foolproof, but it is a bit long, involving nine steps and a variety of alternatives:

1. *The American*, or *Washington Square*, or "The Aspern Papers," or *Daisy Miller* and *The Europeans.*

2. *The Portrait of a Lady*
3. *The Bostonians,* or *The Tragic Muse*
4. Any two of the following short stories: "The Lesson of the Master," "The Death of the Lion," "Greville Fane," "The Abasement of the Northmores," "The Real Thing," "The Liar," "The Altar of the Dead."
5. "The Turn of the Screw," or *The Spoils of Poynton*
6. "The Beast in the Jungle," or "The Jolly Corner"
7. *The Ambassadors*
8. *The Wings of the Dove*
9. *The Golden Bowl*

My second is less sure, but it is for those with less time for fiction:

1. *Washington Square*
2. *The Portrait of a Lady*
3. "The Aspern Papers"
4. "The Turn of the Screw"
5. *The Ambassadors*
6. *The Wings of the Dove*

It would be preferable to add some of the short stories to the second list, but time, I know, is precious. One shudders to consider what James, who found his own era too full of noise and distraction, would have thought of ours. Except one should remember that he loved the typewriter and the automobile. He might have loved the jet plane. It is interesting to ponder the fate of Daisy Miller in a Rome only a few hours by air from Schenectady.

*